THE CAREER BREAK TRAVELER'S HANDBOOK

How to make your dream trip a reality today.

Jeffrey Jung

The Career Break Traveler's Handbook: How to make your dream trip a reality today.

Disclaimer:

This book provides entertaining and informative snapshots of the writer's personal experiences and helpful tips from the writer and others, learned while traveling around the world. The tips provided in this book are not meant to serve as an exclusive checklist to effectively safeguard the reader in every travel situation. Each reader should complete updated, detailed research from legitimate sources to learn the cultural norms and safety recommendations for their specific destination. No one can guarantee safety and travel can expose everyone to potential risks. Because safety is impacted by each person's actions and choices, each reader is advised to always do their homework on their destination and use their best judgment while on their journey.

I wish you safe and happy travels.

For my parents for being my biggest supporters,
for advising me whether I was open to hearing their advice
or not, for listening to me in good times and bad,
and for shaping me into the person I am today.

Acknowledgements

This book is the result of so many good people I've met and my personal journey which began back in 2006. I have to start with my friends Mike and Joy who inadvertently sparked my career break over margaritas and Spanish food. Luckily when I shared the news with my parents, they supported me and even joined me on the road to see South Africa.

My dear friend and business partner, Cheryl, has been with me every step of the way in launching Career Break Secrets. Without her support, advice and humor, and more than a few shared bottles of wine none of this would be possible. I also want to thank Mateo and Liliana for all their hard work and sticking with me. Since starting Career Break Secrets I've had the good fortune to meet people from around the world and hear their stories, further fueling my passion for career breaks and giving me a chance to learn from their experiences.

Thanks to all who generously gave their time to help me with the book. Some shared their stories, some provided constructive criticism, all are appreciated. Finally, thank you to Janice Waugh for giving me the opportunity to publish this book, thereby allowing me to take my career break message to a wider audience.

Contents

Contents

I really got off-the-beaten track when I went 4x4ing on The Southern Highway (La Carretera Austral) in the Chilean Patagonia.

66 *Life moves pretty fast. If you don't stop and look around once in a while, you could miss it.* 99

Ferris Bueller, 1986[1]

The Backstory

Travel has always been a part of my life. When I was eleven years old, my family hosted the first of many foreign exchange students through Rotary International. They came from all over the world - Germany, France, Brazil, New Zealand and Australia - to my little town of Fredericksburg, population 5,000, in the center of Texas. Having foreign brothers and sisters was normal to me. I loved seeing the pictures of their home countries and their families, and hearing the stories about what it was like to live in those places.

Years later, as an exchange student myself in Australia and South Africa, I lived with local host families. I traveled with them, ate with them, saw the countries through their eyes. Traveling as a local was just how everyone traveled, or so I assumed.

Those early experiences shaped not only how I traveled, but also how I sought to understand the world. Why go to a restaurant when you can be in the kitchen with a friend helping them cook and learning about the dish? Why just go to a museum to learn about the local culture and history when you have friends who are part of it?

After college, I jumped into corporate life with both feet. "Do you like to travel?" asked the recruiter who interviewed me.

"I love to travel," I proudly responded. "I've lived overseas and would have no problem taking international assignments." I showed the kind of gung-ho spirit that consulting recruiters love to see. Of course, what I didn't realize was that business travel was completely different. Frequent flier miles were the most tangible rewards that I accumulated from my business travel experiences.

Eventually, I left consulting to join a small, fast growing medical device company. It had a fiercely dynamic culture. Hours were long, management was tough but fair, and I really believed (and still do) in the company's products. I traveled less for work at this time, which allowed me to start developing a personal life.

Yet, as time went on the pressures increased. The business clichés played out before my eyes: more with less, daily fire drill, new sales programs, new projects for greater revenue generation, old projects to finish on time, client meetings, late nights, early mornings, and everything had an urgent deadline. Uh-oh, here comes a reorganization.

Sigh.

When I started the job, "dynamic" meant fun, exciting, challenging, and rewarding. But it came to mean long days, longer nights, and taking work home over the weekend. The life I really wanted for myself was slowly fading away. I became restless, unhappy.

Personal travel during my corporate years was as much for escape as for my love of it. Yes, I went to places I wanted to see. But leaving the country also served as a way to escape the phone calls, e-mails and corporate drama.

"I'll be in South Africa, so I won't have access to messages or e-mail. Sorry!" would say with a smile. Inside, I was thinking, "You can't find me there. Nah nah-nah-nah-nah-nah!"

Childish? Yes. Unprofessional? Perhaps. Necessary for my mental health? Absolutely.

Was this what success meant? Was there no way to be successful at work and lead a balanced life? Had I made a bargain with the devil, building a successful career while sacrificing a satisfying personal life?

If so, I certainly hadn't realized it when I got into the corporate game. With the thrill of professional success gone, how was I ever going to engage with the things that really mattered to me: time for myself, for my family and friends, time to pursue my personal passions?

Then it happened.

What's it going to take to make you happy?"

The margarita glasses sweated profusely in the thick Friday night air on the San Antonio Riverwalk. During dinner, my friends Mike and Joy asked me that fateful question.

It was followed by an uncomfortable pause and the margarita glasses suddenly weren't the only thing sweating. It was a question that I had been asking myself, but I didn't have an answer. I could no longer avoid it. They had my full attention.

> **❝** *What's it going to take to make you happy?* **❞**

Mike and Joy's question rang in my ears like an alarm. The next morning I woke up in every way a person can. I had an epiphany: I wanted to travel.

I wanted to go to all those places that I had been dreaming about since I was a kid. I wanted to travel the way that I did when I was in Australia and South Africa: slowly, getting to know the local culture, making the country my own. I wanted to focus on some of my hobbies that I never seemed able to fit in to my "normal" life. I wanted time for myself and my passions.

To some, it appeared that I was running away. I saw it as a life-enhancing change. If it meant I had to leave my job, I was fine with that.

Then came the questions from within. Was it possible? How could I do it? Was I the only one with this dream? Could I afford it?

Four weeks later, I quit my job and started my new life.

I left a few months later on my career break and had an incredible trip. I started in South America, traveling to Patagonia, Easter Island, Machu Picchu, the Galapagos Islands, Brazil and Colombia. I then headed to Europe and eventually went on to Turkey and Egypt. I fulfilled the goals that I had set ahead of time and accomplished a few things I couldn't have planned.

When I left my job, the term "career break" didn't really exist. But there certainly was a community of people from around the world who were already doing it. In this book, I want to show that a career break is possible for you, how to plan for it, how to get the most out of your time on the road, and how to use your career break to your advantage once you re-enter the workforce.

It may be a bit touristy, but I had fun discovering Colombia's coffee history at the National Coffee Park.

Jeff Jung

DECIDING

It's not hard to make decisions when you know what your values are.

Roy Disney

Discovering the hauntingly barren beauty of the salt flats outside Purmamarca, Argentina is one of my favorite memories from my career break.

The Catalyst

Life can be so hectic that we often find ourselves simply going through the motions. Our routines are built around our work lives. Add in family time, and there's precious little time left for yourself.

What's the net result? We forget that we can choose how we live our lives. We forget that we have the choice, and even the responsibility, to live the life that we want and need. Many career breakers I talk to (and it's true of me as well) tell me that they lost sight of this at some point along the way. What all career breakers have in common is a memorable moment - a jolt - that reminded them of who they really wanted to be, and that shook them out of their inertia.

That jolt is what I call the catalyst.

For me, it was a simple question posed at the right time by the right people: what would it take to make me happy? Strong emotions are often part of the mix. A career break catalyst is so powerful that it shakes you out of your current state and forces you to look at your life and take action.

World travel had always been on my mind and something I intended to tackle someday. But the pointed conversation with good friends that I recounted in my back story suddenly brought my dream to the forefront and imbued it with a sense of urgency.

Catalytic moments are not why you go. They are what prompt you to action. Here are a few common ones:

- change of job status
- change of relationship status
- burnout
- loss of a loved one
- desire to make a life change
- an already occurring life change

Who Takes Career Breaks? Catherine:
Facing Down a Health Threat then Celebrating Life

In October of 2008, I was young, twenty-three years old, healthy and content, safely coasting through life in a corporate marketing job and in a long-term relationship. According to the measures of success around me, I thought things were as they should be. Then, out of the blue, I was told that I had a benign brain tumor. I finally understood what it meant to realize that our lives are unpredictable and often out of our control.

Although it was not life-threatening and could be controlled with medication, the lasting impact of that moment of uncertainty changed my mindset and my outlook on how I was living my life for good. I decided to turn my "I've always wanted to..." list into a "to-do" list and immediately began mapping out how to make those things come to fruition. One of the top items on my list had always been to live abroad, so I stopped coming up with excuses for why I shouldn't do it, and instead started detailing how I could make it happen. I soon quit my corporate job that I had no passion for, ended an unhealthy relationship, and found temporary jobs and ways to save money on living expenses in order to fund my trip.

Within one year, I moved to Argentina and spent a life-changing nine months traveling through South America, studying Spanish, and working with people from around the world. Deciding to take charge of my destiny ignited a new desire within me – to help others take the same step towards pursuing their dreams, but without having to experience a "wake-up call" life event.

Catherine is now a goals coach in Austin, Texas helping others pursue and achieve their goals and dreams, whether related to health and wellness, personal life or career, so they may live joyful, abundant and fulfilling lives. She can be contacted at Thrive-ing.com

What We Can Learn from Pro Athletes

Most of us do not have physically demanding jobs. Ours are more mentally and emotionally taxing. Our stress comes from the deadlines, projects, and people - customers, patients or students - that we have to manage or work with. In other words, most of us are stressed by daily mental challenges.

Once you leave your job at night, do you take time to work off that stress by maintaining a proper work-life balance? Do you work out like you should? Go for a stress-reducing massage? Engage in hobbies? Spend enough time with family and friends?

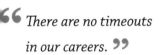

> **66** *There are no timeouts in our careers.* **99**

Many of us end the day without de-stressing properly. Then, the next day, we go right back into the environment that caused that stress in the first place.

To a certain extent, we accept this. It's part of the working contract between employer and employee. It's normal for there to be ebbs and flows in our workload. But what happens when the balance becomes so out of whack that you are constantly consumed by work and you can't turn it off?

Well, there's vacation, right?

In theory, yes, but often you are expected to be available via e-mail and voicemail while away. Further, there's a disturbing trend, at least in the US, in which people aren't even taking vacations. When did companies become so fragile that the loss of one employee for a week or two could single-handedly cause their collapse?

Makes you want to throw a penalty flag at your boss, doesn't it?

Pro athletes are finely tuned physical machines. They are expected to give 110% on the field. One mistake could cost them or their team the game.

But off the field, they relax! They get physical therapy. Yes, they train and maintain themselves to keep up with the high level of intensity on the field. But they also rest and rejuvenate so as not to over-stress their bodies. Finally, pro athletes get an off-season to prepare for the next one.

The stress put on pro athletes is physically evident. The stress created in our jobs is not. Yet stress is there nonetheless. Let's learn from the pros and take care of ourselves when not at work. We have to make time to rejuvenate and create our own off-season.

Just hanging out in the Salta region of Argentina.

The 3% Perspective - Why a Career Break Is Not Selfish

There may not be universal acceptance, but the tide is turning in favor of a break being a normal part of one's career. Two leading career experts share their perspectives.

The world of work is changing as we speak. In spite of high unemployment, individuals are claiming their free agency status by seeking and creating work that is more fulfilling and leverages their true competencies. Meanwhile, organizations are adapting to the needs and demands of valuable workers, which includes taking career breaks, self-directed vacations, etc. These and other arrangements are designed to derive an optimal work product from these employees and workers.

Ginny Clarke, CEO of Talent Optimization Partners and author of
Career Mapping: Charting Your Course in the New World of Work.

It used to be that someone who took time off to pursue an interest outside of work was viewed with suspicion, or at the very least seen as "not serious about his career." Even in those supposed good old days, I think there was an element of envy or curiosity on the part of the hiring managers, as in "I wish I could do that, too!" Without a doubt, that thinking has evolved, and as the old thinking continues to retire from the workforce, the evolution will continue into accepted, maybe even encouraged practice. It is no secret that as humans, we are the product of our experiences. And smart employers know that they are hiring the whole human, not just the "related work experience" part. Each of us must start thinking of our lives, and our careers, in terms of the experiences we are collecting. Are we living the experiences we want to live? If not, why not? Big questions require big answers - not all of them easy.

Julie Bauke, CEO, The Bauke Group and author of
Stop Peeing on Your Shoes: Avoiding the 7 Mistakes That Screw Up Your Job Search.

Back in college, my advisers universally proclaimed that my career would be composed of multiple employers. The one-employer career was going away. They were right. With few exceptions, my friends, family, and I have all experienced this.

So, given the state of our career paths, is it really so odd to slip in a three-, six- or twelve-month planned career break between jobs?

> 66 *Is it really too much to ask that you take less than 3 percent of your adult life to focus on you?* 99

Look at it another way. How many years will you spend working during your adult life? To keep the math simple, let's say forty years, starting at the age of twenty-five and retiring at sixty-five. That equals 480 months of full employment. If you take a career break for three, six or twelve months, that works out to 0.625 percent, 1.25 percent or 2.5 percent of your adult working years. Is it really too much to ask that you take less than 3 percent of your adult life to focus on you?

From that perspective, a career break isn't selfish.

With limited vacation time, we can't see all the places in the world we want to see. It's unlikely that you will be able to hike the Annapurna Circuit in Nepal, go to the deepest pockets of Patagonia, or travel overland in eastern Africa. You need a career break to make your travel dreams possible.

But a career break is not just about travel and fun. It's an active time in your life. It presents the opportunity to give back by volunteering. It's a time for gathering new skills and experiences to enrich your life and your contribution at work. It's about understanding the world better.

You only get one shot at life. Are you really sure you can't take less than 3 percent of your working life to do what you want to do, to reconnect with yourself and pursue personal passions?

Who Takes Career Breaks? Warren & Betsy:
From Personal Losses to Lives Regained

Margaritas, friends, and an unexpected question were the perfect combination to change our lives.

In retrospect the evening started like any other great night out. We were celebrating a long weekend in Seattle and decided to head out to our favorite Mexican restaurant with close friends. These are the types of friends where a conversation just flows and there are no restrictions. We all felt free to share ideas, hopes, and concerns with each other.

As the hours wore on, Betsy and I started to reflect on our friends and family. Betsy's brother was still managing life after a major heart attack at age thirty-five. While he had recovered, it had required a major shift in diet and attitude. Our close friend Maria was still in the hospital almost one month after a brain aneurysm at age thirty-four and no one knew what the future held. Without even knowing it, our lives were about to be changed.

As typically happens with great friends the discussion turned to life and the future. We reflected on how short life is and posed the question, "What would you do if you knew you would not live to be forty?" (we were both thirty-seven at the time).

Without pausing to consult, Betsy and I both answered, "Travel."

Within an hour, and thanks to the aid of another round of margaritas, we had made the decision that would change our lives. We had agreed that we would take a year off to travel around the world. The next morning, in the cold light of day, we knew that our mindset had been changed forever and we started planning our adventure in earnest.

Warren and Betsy are currently traveling the world. Through their books and their website, MarriedWithLuggage.com, they help others create their perfect lives.

The Emerging Science Behind Career Breaks and Sabbaticals

"Sabbatical leave promotes well-being." That is the bottom-line conclusion of a recent academic study, *Sabbatical Leave: Who Gains and How Much?*, which was conducted by researchers from the US, Israel and New Zealand.[2] The study measured the effects of a sabbatical on a person's health and well-being.

The conclusion was supported by the study's key findings (translated into layperson's terms).

- Stress decreases during a career break. Even though it comes back after returning to work, the level of stress is lower than before the break.
- Life satisfaction increases during the sabbatical but returns to "normal" over time after the break.
- People who adapt well to new environments got over burnout more easily and suffered less from burnout after the career break.
- Those who believe they are more in control of their lives benefitted even more from their sabbatical.
- Those who detached more from their life at home experienced greater relief from stress and burnout and derived more satisfaction from their career break. Furthermore, these people suffered less from stress and burnout after returning to work.
- Those who spent time abroad during their break experienced higher levels of rejuvenation than those who stayed in their home country.

So what does this mean for you?

- **Go for it.** Take the break! If you've been wondering if taking a break can really be that great, there is now a growing body of evidence that shows that it can be. If you are suffering from burnout, need to cut work-related stress or simply have the travel bug and want to reconnect with your personal passions, a career break is your answer.
- **Be in control, but don't be a control freak.** The act of taking time off from your career is an important step in resuming control of your life. You

will be taking the time to do the things that you want to do, the things that you need to do. Set clear goals, then be flexible in how you work towards achieving them. You do yourself no favors by trying to control everything tightly.

- **The more you leave behind, the better.** The more you can leave behind, the more you will get out of your time off. A career break isn't about becoming irresponsible. It's about allowing yourself to focus on the things that you need to do in your life while you see the world.

- **Go overseas.** There's a whole world to see. So, take some time to go out and experience part of it. Chances are, if you have a bit of the travel bug, there's something you've always wanted to do or someplace you've always wanted to see. A career break trip is the perfect time to do it.

spent four days exploring the mystery and mysticism of the Rapa Nui culture on Easter sland and the moai they left behind.

Who Takes Career Breaks? Caroline & Chris:
A Routine Call Leads to a Change of Routine

I was done. The corporate world had taken the best of me. My sense of humor, my joie de vivre, and my laid-back personality were all but a distant memory. It came to a head on a regular day in April, 1999. It was hot, I was stuck in Austin traffic, and I got a call from an angry client. It wasn't anything I couldn't handle, but for some reason, that day, I couldn't take it. I hung up the phone and thought, I'm out of here.

A month later, my best friend Chris and I were enjoying happy hour at a local bar. I told her how I felt and she and I decided it was time. It was time to quit our jobs and take a trip around the world. We would chase summer for a full year, see the developing world, and create an adventure of a lifetime. The following January, we left and fulfilled our dream.

After a transformative experience while volunteering in India, Caroline founded The Miracle Foundation, a non-profit organization that partners with orphanages throughout India to help orphans reach their full potential. Chris runs her own real estate company, HotAustinRealEstate.com.

Dealing with the Mental Hurdles of Leaving

Despite all of your enthusiasm for taking a career break, saying goodbye is always tough. Mental hurdles will arise to challenge your plans. When they do, it is important to maintain perspective about the change you are making in your life. This is simply a transition to another life stage. Transitions are normal. Some are dramatic, many are quiet. You've been through a lot of them. Think back two, three or five years. Think about how much your life has changed.

With this transition you're going away for a while. For most people, this is simply a break: nothing more, nothing less. This perspective is critical when the mental hurdles of leaving start to appear. Here are just a few you may face:

I should wait for the right time. There is always a reason to stay. Unless your catalyst was an already occurring life event, it can feel like there will never be a good time to go. Be strategic about when you leave but don't wait for the perfect time.

Maybe this is a bad idea, no one is supporting me. Keep in mind that this is your dream, not necessarily that of others in your life. They may not understand or be supportive. They may not want to understand. They will need time to adjust to the fact that you're going away for a little while. Be patient.

It's too overwhelming. There is a lot to deal with in taking a career break. Breathe. Relax. Remember that you have dealt with stress and change before. You can do this. Most career breakers take at least six months to plan and prepare. Take it one step at a time.

There's so much I don't know. For many of us, upending our lives to go travel for an extended period of time can be intimidating. Have confidence in yourself and your ability to cope and thrive. After all, it's what made you successful at your career. Tap into the online career break community for inspiration and advice.

My current situation isn't really so bad. Sometimes in moments of immense change, we look back at the status quo and rationalize that things are fine, that change isn't necessary. Don't lose sight of the reasons that you sought to undertake this journey.

Who Takes Career Breaks? Angela: *Expanding Personal Horizons During an Economic Downturn*

I stepped out in faith and quit my job in the midst of the 2009 recession to follow my dream. My "aha" moment came when I realized that I would rather take a chance on myself than continue the daily grind. At the age of forty, selling my stuff was not an option. But when that nagging feeling to take a sabbatical would not go away, I knew that I had to take action. So I prayed, reviewed my finances, and made my break.

When I quit, I had no clue what was next. But a few days later, I was on a plane going to Italy!

Who knew that three years and thirty countries later I would have flown an airplane, stared in awe at the Pyramids of Giza, narrowly escaped the earthquake in Japan, and be pursuing a doctorate in organizational leadership? Where will your dreams take you?

Angela is now working towards her doctorate in organizational leadership in Houston, Texas and continues to write about her travels on SabbaticalScapes.com.

A Final Pep Talk to Get You Going

The fact that you are reading this book means that you have more than a passing desire to take your dream trip. Maybe you've already had your catalytic moment. Perhaps it's still coming.

There's often a short period at the beginning in which you may find yourself on an emotional roller coaster. One day you feel 100 percent certain of your decision to go. The next day, the mental hurdles block your way. If this happens to you, I want you to come back to this page and reread the points below to get yourself focused again.

Focus on what you are running to during your break. This is not a time to run away. It's a time to run to something. Focus on what that goal is and let that be your guide.

Remember that this will be an active trip. This will not be a time for you to sit on the couch. You will be traveling around taking in the sights. Slowing down, yes. But you will be refocusing your energies in a new way, towards your personal passions. That will keep you active and relaxed, and give you lasting memories and accomplishments to show off once you return.

Remember that you're not the only one. It's quite possible that you don't know a single person in your inner circle who has taken a break. That's already changed: now you know me. The advice given in this book represents the accumulation of knowledge that I've gained from my own trip and from meeting hundreds of other career breakers. I will share that knowledge with you and introduce you to the career break community so you can start meeting these people for yourself.

Give yourself permission. You are the only one you need it from. This is your life, and these are your choices. You will live with the benefits and consequences of having taken the trip. You have to live with yourself and look at yourself in the mirror every day. Live your life for you, not for anyone else.

Embrace Peace of Mind Planning. There are lots of things you can do to make it easier to transition into and out of your career break. Good planning is essential and we'll tackle this.

Finally, you have something in you that has already brought you success in your life. You can figure out the blocking and tackling of getting ready. You're going to have a great trip! And when you get back, you will have that success as your starting point to resume your career. Plus, your personal goals will have been accomplished, your passions will have been rekindled, you will have made a new circle of friends, and it will all have happened because you gave yourself permission to go, and prepared yourself with proper planning.

I came into contact with cultures and histories I never knew existed before my career break including pre-Colombian history at the Gold Museum in Bogotá, Colombia.

Should I Stay or Should I Go?

This story was written by Janice Waugh and excerpted from SoloTravelerBlog.com

My husband had traveled for a year through South America when I was just entering high school (he had seven years on me). I had taken many short trips since I was fifteen years old – a few weeks here, a month there. Together, as we blended our families, started and built a business – we lived a very busy life – we also planned to travel. In 1995, we managed six weeks with our kids in France, Scotland, and Ireland. But that wasn't enough. We had bigger plans in mind.

Then, in 2000, it seemed right. Our number three son could complete his last year at Neuchatel Junior College in Switzerland, and I would homeschool our youngest. We could rent our house for income and rent a VW Pop-up camper for transportation and accommodation. We fit the pieces together and left at the end of August, 2001.

Over the next ten months we covered a lot of ground. My mother joined us for a few weeks. The older sons each came over for a time. It was a free-flowing trip of a lifetime. When we needed to, we stayed. When we'd had enough, we simply moved on.

We came home in June of 2002, which is a perfect time to return. The summer is slower and it gave us two months to prepare for the real new year, September. However, while the kids and I settled back into our home life, my husband became less settled. Was it the culture shock of re-entry? We couldn't tell at first but his life, our life, got very complicated.

In 2006, my husband was diagnosed with Progressive Supranuclear Palsy (PSP), a very rare neurological disease that first shows itself in personality changes and later with debilitating physical changes. He passed away later that year.

While our choice to take an extended trip at that particular time of life may have seemed odd to some, we made it make sense. We put our present and our future on a scale and chose to live in the present for that year. And, at the time, we had no idea that it was our last chance to do so.

Should you stay or should you go? Go.

Jeff Jung

PEACE
OF MIND
PLANNING

*Someone's sitting in the shade
today because someone planted
a tree a long time ago.*

Warren Buffett

Proper planning will ensure that you can enjoy unexpected moments. Here's one I experienced while visiting the Taj Mahal as I turned back towards the entrance.

A Difficult but Necessary Conversation

Before I left for my trip, I sat down with my parents. It was going to be a tough conversation that none of us were looking forward to having. This was not a conversation that many kids have with their parents. But there was no avoiding it. We sat around the dining room table and slowly I went through it all: my will, my living will, my finances, my health insurance and repatriation information, important addresses, phone numbers, and power of attorney.

It wasn't pleasant. But if something was going to happen to me, I wanted to minimize the stress involved for my parents in managing my affairs and minimize the number of decisions that they would have to make. I created a trust to manage my financial affairs, a living will to spell out my health decisions, and purchased repatriation insurance coverage to get me back home as easily as possible if I died. Mom shed a few tears as we went through everything, but at the end we all felt better having gone through the exercise.

Peace of Mind Career Break Planning Overview

Your planning goal is to ensure your peace of mind while you travel. Peace of Mind Planning is about reducing or eliminating risks - financial, safety and security, career, and health - and liberating yourself to live in the moment as you travel.

Essentially, you want to ensure that:

- your finances are sound during and after your trip
- you have planned for contingencies in case of emergencies
- your belongings are secured
- you are prepared to re-enter the job market
- you are free to live in the moment while you travel

There are two components to Peace of Mind Planning.

1. Over-plan what you leave behind. Minimize your worries and responsibilities back home so you can let go and enjoy your trip.

For the issues that are known in advance, you can have a specific remedy in place. For example, you need to ensure your cash flow while traveling so you will need to plan to have the right financial instruments at your disposal.

> 66 *For probably the first time in your life, you are going to have more time than money during your trip. Allow yourself the luxury of slowing down.* 99

For issues that can't be foreseen, for example, if you lose your stuff, you need to have processes procedures, backup plans and responsible parties in place in order to deal with them.

Having a good plan frees you up to enjoy your trip, live in the moment, and be spontaneous about where you travel and what you do. After all, you want to make your career break count, enjoy your time while traveling, and achieve your goals.

2. Under-plan your travel itinerary.

For probably the first time in your life, you are going to have more time than money during your trip. Allow yourself the luxury of slowing down. When you get to a new country, you are going to discover places and things to do that you couldn't have planned for. Flexibility allows you to be spontaneous and live in the moment without taking away from your overall goals.

At the same time, as you get into your trip planning, you will realize that three months, six months, even twelve months traveling will pass quickly. Focus on what you really want to see and do. Determining these goals will give you the basic boundaries or structure for your trip. This is your starting point.

To get focused, answer this:

The three most important things for me to see and/or do on my career break are:

1. _____
2. _____
3. _____

Once you've gone through this exercise, these will be the big markers in your itinerary. For everything else, let go and enjoy the opportunities that come your way.

It may be blurry, but this photo in the Amazon reminds me of how my career break helped me learn to live in the moment again.

Coming Out of the Career Break Closet

Once I decided that I wanted a break to travel, I couldn't stop planning and thinking about it. It consumed me. I spent every free moment researching a new destination, recalculating my route or refining my budget. It was exhilarating. I was obsessed. The only problem was that I couldn't tell anyone. Not yet.

I was like that little kid who knows what his sister is getting for her birthday but can't tell. I had a goofy smile on my face at work. I was relaxed. Because I knew I was on a path to change my life, I was able to put my job into proper perspective. I stopped taking everything so seriously, or personally.

I went into my friend Mike's office and closed the door (the same Mike who had asked me what would make me happy). He saw that I had some news. The smirk on my face betrayed me. He smiled, let out a laugh, and asked, "What?"

What he was really asking was, "What have you done?"

We spoke for a while. I told him that I was going to be leaving to travel. It took him aback. He made his case about why I should not leave my job at the moment and why I should take more time to think it over. He wasn't saying "Don't do it," but he was saying "Don't do it now."

"Uh-oh," I thought, "I could be in for a bumpy ride as I let people know."

While taking a career break has started to become less of an oddity, you probably don't know many people who have done it. That can cause stress and anxiety. Will people think I'm crazy? Will they think I've lost it?

We all worry about what our friends and family will think. We all fear their response. But that's not a reason to keep you from fulfilling your dream. Here are a few of the reactions you might encounter.

Concern. Social norms are powerful forces in our lives. When we deviate from them, people can have an initial knee-jerk response of "What's wrong? Is everything OK?" It's not that they can't learn or be educated, but that acceptance and support don't always come naturally at first.

Fear projection. For many people, traveling the world, exploring a country in depth, and leaving their life behind for a period of time inspires fear, not intrigue. These people won't be able to understand how or why this could be your dream.

Jealousy. I know one career breaker whose mother was extremely upset when she told her about her plans, causing tension in their relationship for a prolonged period of time. Later, her father confided in her that world travel had been her mom's dream, but it had never panned out. Sadly, rather than support her daughter, the mom acted out. There can also be another, more positive side to the jealousy. People will come up to you, pull you aside or whisper in your ear telling you how jealous they are of you and your decision. They'll tell you how they wish they had the courage to do what you're doing, and how excited they are to follow you and live vicariously through your adventures.

Condescension and passive-aggressiveness. "What are you running away from?" "Good luck finding yourself." "Why are you being so selfish?" Sigh. It doesn't occur to these people that maybe, just maybe, you're running to something. Maybe your decision to take a career break is the result of having found yourself already. As a result, you're pivoting towards something new. A career break is not an excuse or a cover to run away from your life or your problems. If you are running away, you are doing it wrong. Reflection, yes. Avoidance, no.

Support. Here's the good news. Many, if not most, of the people in your life will support you. On one of my final days before leaving my job, the vice president of sales came into my office. That never happened. If he wanted me, I always went to his office. We sat at my office table, and with a big smile on his face, he started asking me about my trip plans. He was genuinely interested.

Recognize the negative reactions for what they are. The people around you are dealing with the fact that they are going to lose you for a period of time. Some of them will need time to come around. It's exciting to you because you're about to embark on a huge adventure. But it's happening to you, not to them. Give those who are snarky or critical some time to deal with their emotions and you will find that many will come around.

Five Things to Do before You Quit

The thrill of an upcoming career break adventure may be matched only by the anxiety of prepping for it. Before you can get on the road and start relaxing and rebalancing, there are lots of things to take care of, and many details about your life and your trip to get in order.   Don't quit your job until you've completed everything on this list.

Hopefully you will be leaving on good terms, but you should know that some employers have trouble dealing with people quitting. Although you may not be planning to burn any bridges before you leave (even if you secretly want to) you can't predict how your boss will react. Depending on your position within the organization, company policy may require you to leave immediately after resigning. Be prepared for the worst, even if it doesn't come to pass.

1. **Check your company's leave policy.** There may be a policy that allows you to take extended paid or unpaid leave and still keep your job, maybe even your current position. At a minimum, you'll be well informed about your company's policies before you talk to your employer.

2. **Role-play your talk with your boss.** You're going to talk to your boss about taking time off to travel. Maybe your goal is to negotiate your time off. Maybe you are going in simply to give your two week's notice. Whatever your plan, make sure you think through all the possible reactions and have your responses ready. Your boss might simply be curious about your plans, so think about what you are prepared to share

Possible responses from your boss:
- No
- Yes, but not now
- Yes
- Yes, and leave immediately

3. **Get your finances in order.** Of utmost importance are the following points:
   - Pay off your debt. This may be the most obvious one. Don't service a debt while you're traveling.
   - Get two credit cards, one being a Visa.
   - Create your budget. More on this later in this section.
   - Create or update your will.

4. **Get your health in order.** You're still employed, which means you may get your health insurance through your employer. Take advantage of that coverage to get yourself ready for your trip.
   - Get your medical check-ups.
   - Get your shots. Know that some insurance plans won't pay for travel vaccinations.
   - Spend your Flexible Spending Account (FSA) before you quit (US only).
   - Investigate travel health insurance.
   - Stock up on extra medications, contact lenses, etc. as needed.

5. **Update your résumé and portfolio.** You're taking a career break because you have a career to break from. You have many accomplishments and important details that will make you attractive to your next employer after your break. So take the time now, while they are fresh in your mind, to update your résumé.

Finally, to reiterate an important point, don't burn bridges, no matter how much you may want to or feel justified in doing so. Remember, this is the last impression you will leave with your colleagues and employer. Leave them eager to welcome you back to your career after your break.

After seeing your first dramatic landscapes like the cliffs in western Ireland, you won't be thinking about your old job. So, wrap up the details before you go.

Who Takes Career Breaks? Sherry:
Project Planning an Open-Ended Adventure

Since I was a novice traveler having just acquired my first passport at the age of thirty, I had no idea how I was actually going to take this giant leap into the unknown. At a time when I should have been super excited about the prospect of quitting my job and traveling around the world for a year, I was instead stressed out and often driven to tears because of my fears of this unknown journey I was about to take.

I coped by doing what I knew how to do: I made a project plan and started to break everything into digestible bits for my Type A personality. But I stayed motivated by relying on other's excitement for me. I remember telling friends what I was about to do and feeding off of their excitement (and sometimes envy) for me. I used others to keep me motivated and on track, and eventually to push me onto the plane with a passport in desperate need of stamps.

Sherry is still traveling around the world after six years and has dedicated herself to helping others take a career break via MeetPlanGo.com

The Art of Career Break Budgeting in Four Steps

One of the most important questions people ask me is how to afford a break to travel. There's no magic, but there is budgeting. Think of it like a game: how much can you get out of the money that you have?

This process takes the daunting task of budgeting for a long-term trip and breaks it down into bite-sized chunks. Budgeting is a process, not a destination. It is iterative, based on a series of assumptions that will change as you work through it and discover new information.

There are four steps to preparing your budget:

1. Develop initial scenarios for how much money you might need.
2. Develop your pre-takeoff budget.
3. Develop your on-the-road budget.
4. Develop your re-entry budget.

The first step is a high-level analysis designed to give you a sense of how much money you will need during your break and a way to compare it with what you actually have now. The remaining steps are really subsets of your actual budget. As there are discrete stages in the cycle of your career break, so should there be corresponding parts to your career break budget.

Ready? Of course you are!

Step 1: Scenario Playing Your Budget

As I stated above, the goal of scenario playing is to get an idea of how much money you might need. It is the first step to determining the financial feasibility of your trip. I call it scenario playing, and not planning, because at this step the numbers aren't real. They represent potential future needs. You can see what it would cost at your most frugal or most extravagant spending levels. Don't worry, you'll refine the numbers with better estimates later.

When I decided that I really wanted to travel, I focused on trying to figure out if I could afford it. I spent hours conducting online research in an effort to determine costs and budget numbers. But in 2006, there were very few publicly available budget examples. Scenario playing was how I started my own budgeting process.

Calculate Your Daily Lifestyle Costs

The most common way to look at travel budgets is on a per-day basis, so that's how we'll talk about it here. Since it will always be difficult to know what your true costs on the road will be, let's start with what you do know: how much your current lifestyle costs. This is your lifestyle at 100 percent. It's an analysis of what you spend your money on right now. So grab a piece of paper or your favorite spreadsheet and total up your monthly expenses. Don't leave anything out: mortgage/rent, bills, entertainment, gym, those daily lattes, and any pampering you might treat yourself to. Throw it all in.

Now, take that number and divide it by 30, which will take your monthly total to a daily number. You didn't know you were so expensive to maintain, did you? I certainly didn't.

There's an alternative way to do this that's quicker. Take your annual after-tax salary and divide it by 365 to get your daily rate. To give you a range, here are a few basic calculations.

Annual After-Tax Salary	Days in the Year	Daily Cost
$ 30,000.00	365	82.19
$ 40,000.00	365	109.59
$ 60,000.00	365	164.38

If your after-tax income is $30,000/year, you spend about $82 a day to live. For the record, most long-term travelers average less than that while on the road, unless they are traveling in the more expensive destinations in the world.

Create Budget Scenarios

This is where the fun begins. Seriously. Calculate scenarios about how much you think you could live on while on the road. Could you live on 50 percent of your current daily rate from Step 1? Thirty percent? Sixty percent? This exercise will start to give you an idea of the ranges of daily budgets that you will want to set for yourself.

To make this number more real, start looking at your expenses and see what goes away. Are there expenses that you will not be incurring while you're traveling? Of course, there will be many - but there may be some new ones as well. For example, while you may get rid of your apartment or plan to sell your house, you may incur storage fees which you currently don't have.

For me, this was the point at which I decided to get rid of a lot of my possessions. After all, why pay for things back home that I wouldn't be using on the road? Instead, I used that money for extra perks or tours while traveling.

Evaluate Your Savings

Now you have some baseline daily rates for your budget. How long do you plan to be gone? Thirty days? Ninety? Six months? More?

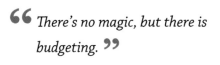

> **" There's no magic, but there is budgeting. "**

To be conservative, include the number of days that you will be unemployed before and after your trip. You want to build in a cushion so that you won't have to worry about money once you return. Adding this cushion will also reduce the chances that you will have to leap at the first job that comes along, especially if it's not one that you want.

Let's do the math together. In this example, you will have thirty days between leaving your job and getting on a plane, sixty days for travel, and sixty days for job hunting upon your return. Your at-home budget will be $82 per day and your travel budget will be $50 per day. The calculation is simply this:

$$(30 \text{ days X } \$82) + (60 \text{ days X } \$50) + (60 \text{ days X } \$82) = \$10,380.$$

That's the rough amount that you want to have in savings for your trip. Compare that to what you already have. Do you have enough? Are you short? Are you close?

Play, Revise and Refine

Since you're scenario playing, change the daily costs and days of travel to work out a range of possible budgets. Granted, these numbers aren't real. But this exercise will stimulate your thinking about what kind of trip you could have and how to finance it. It will also get you thinking about specific expenses like plane tickets, insurance, vaccinations, etc., and how you will budget for those items.

In my case, once I performed these calculations, I realized that I already had the savings to finance the trip, and it made my decision to take a career break much easier. There was still work to do, but I knew I was in the ballpark.

Keep this analysis handy. As you go through the rest of the budgeting exercise, you will have more information and data to continue refining it.

Step 2: Pre-Takeoff Budgeting

Now that you have initial budget ranges and a general idea of how much you will need to finance your trip, it's time to get specific, or as specific as possible at this point. This is why I call it the art, not the science, of budgeting.

The Pre-Takeoff Budget, as its name implies, simply covers the time between leaving your job and getting on the plane. As I mentioned in the previous section, your starting budget baseline is equal to your current daily spend (hint, that number from Step 1).

To gain more specificity, there are three factors that you need to consider in determining how much money you will need for this part of your budget.

1. **How much time will you have between quitting your job and leaving?**
   Some people leave mere weeks after they quit. Others want a little more

time. Whatever your timeframe, it's best to set your daily budget high. For budgeting and saving purposes, assume that you need as much to live on as you did while you still had a job. If you can economize a bit during this period, then you'll have a nice cushion for your trip or for your re-entry period.

Smart budgeting will help you indulge in an occasional splurge on the road. I didn't stay at Casapueblo in Uruguay, but I did enjoy a few luxuries from time to time.

2. **How much do you need to buy for your trip?** Do you already have a backpack or luggage? Do you already have the basic clothing and gear? Or are you starting from scratch? The more you've traveled before, in theory, the less you will need to spend. Then again, you may be tempted to replace some of your gear just because of the importance of this trip.

3. **How many costs can you incur in this phase?** Some of the items on the checklists in this phase and the next are interchangeable depending on your preferences. For example, are you buying a full round-the-world ticket

or is your goal to get to your first destination and take it from there? The more you spend before you leave, the less you need to spend on the road. This is an accounting decision for you to make, not a recommendation to incur expenses before it's necessary to do so.

Budget Categories for Your Pre-Takeoff Budget

Here is a starter list to help you get organized.

- **Home:** mortgage/rent, utilities, insurance, food
- **Finances:** setting up/updating your will, trust, credit cards, debit cards
- **Clothing:** pants, wool socks, hiking boots, flip flops, things you can layer. Side note: think breathable and quick drying fabrics as much as possible.
- **Gear:** backpack, headlamp, travel towel, water bottle, sports watch (I actually stopped wearing a watch while traveling, but I know a lot of people who still like to have one.)
- **Electronics:** laptop/netbook, iPod, unlocked cell phone, e-reader/tablet
- **Other travel items:** tickets, hostel membership, day or extended tours, visa fees, guides, airport lounge memberships
- **Health items:** vaccinations, doctor and dental visits, glasses, contact lenses, travel health insurance, health insurance to cover you while still in your home country, small first aid kit/supplies, medicines
- **Entertainment:** books, music, movies

Step 3: On-the-Road Travel Budget

Travel the world for $20, $30, or $50 a day. It's so hard to know how much you really need until you get there. But that's little consolation when you're trying to make sure you have enough put aside.

No one can tell you how much you will need. For all I know, you may need a four-star hotel every night and you have no desire to take a local bus. To get started in planning this part of your budget, use the following categories to think through what you will need. Then, refer to the end of the book for additional resources to help you continue refining your budget.

Here are a few factors to take into consideration.

- **Budget Traveler?** How much of a budget traveler are you? Everyone is on a budget when they travel. In fact, most people I've met consider themselves to be budget travelers. But there's budget travel and then there is $5/night in a dorm with 18 other people budget travel. Some are willing to stay at a two-star hotel, while others will couchsurf. Whatever kind of traveler you are, be honest with yourself and budget accordingly.

- **Back Home Expenses:** Your goal is to minimize as much of your responsibility back home as possible. It will reduce your worry and the number of items that you have to budget for. Leave as few financial obligations behind as possible, such as:
  - mortgage/rent
  - insurance: home, car
  - storage
  - debt, loans
  - utilities

- **Eating Habits:** You'll no doubt be eating out while you're traveling. It's unavoidable and one of the great pleasures of travel. But, if you can cook a few meals for yourself, you'll save money on the road. Consider the costs of:
  - restaurants
  - markets/grocers
  - special dietary needs or restrictions

- **Accommodation:** Before I left on my trip, a good friend who had taken a career break told me, "Jeff, sometimes you're just going to want a hotel." She was right. But for the vast majority of the time, more modest selections will be your choice:
  - hostels
  - apartments
  - pensiones
  - house sitting

- **Transportation:** Here are a couple of tips about foreign airlines:
  - Pricing systems differ. Not all foreign airlines have pricing structures that cause the price to go up closer to the departure date. You can sometimes get a good deal at the last minute.
  - Beware of budget airlines. The cheapest ticket isn't always the cheapest flight if there are a lot of ancillary fees. I flew RyanAir once. It cost me a fortune after the charges were added, baggage fees being only one of them.

Finally, how will you get around in the cities and towns you visit? The more overland transport you can take, the cheaper it will be. The challenge in budgeting for this is that bus and train prices are difficult to research ahead of time. But maximizing the use of local transportation and minimizing taxi use will stretch your budget. And, of course, walking, when possible, costs nothing. Consider the cost of:
  - planes
  - trains
  - buses
  - automobiles
  - taxis
  - rickshaws

- **Bank fees:** There are a couple of key fees to investigate: ATM charges and foreign transaction fees on credit cards. Shop around to get the best deals. These will add up over time, so choose wisely:
  - currency exchange fees
  - ATM fees
  - credit card foreign transaction fees
  - monthly banking fees

- **Other items to remember:**
  - health insurance – if not already accounted for in your Pre-Takeoff Budget
  - tours
  - tips
  - medicines and doctor visits
  - communication needs: SIM cards, phone and/or Internet
  - entry visa fees
  - entertainment
  - books, magazines, newspapers
  - music, movies
  - gifts and market shopping
  - splurges like an occasional spa day or a nice meal
  - travel guides
  - replacement clothes
  - emergency funds
  - baggage fees (another reason to pack light)

Step 4: Re-entry Budget

The final part of your budget covers the re-entry stage. This is the easiest part of the budget to calculate. The formula is simply:

Average daily spend X the number of days before earning a salary

Here are a few factors to think about as you set your budget.

- Will there be a job waiting for you?
- How are the general economic conditions?
- What will your living costs be?
- Will you have moving expenses? Are you returning to the same city or are you going to be starting fresh somewhere else?
- Are you planning a career change or continuing in the same field?

Generally speaking, if you are going to be staying in the same career or profession, your search time for a new job will be shorter. Why? All of your contacts, expertise, and know-how are in that industry.

If you are looking to change careers, you should plan for it to take longer. Why? You are starting over without a support structure or industry colleagues to help guide your way. This might be shortened if you used part of your career break to build some skills or knowledge in this new area. Either way, it will impact your search time.

Flexibility gives you the chance to live in the moment. I took an unexpected road trip through Northwestern Argentina on a whim with some great travelers I met in a bus station.

Getting Your Finances in Order

Having your finances in order means more than just having the cash saved for your trip. You must be able to access your money, manage it, pay your bills with it and protect your digital identity while traveling. Again, for peace of mind, set everything up before you go. Once you're on the road, it's going to be more difficult to resolve.

Here is a list of things that you need to do before you head for the airport:

Banking

Start by determining if your bank can meet your needs. Not all banks have great international networks. It might be best to switch banks, or at least open an account with a more global bank.

Once you've selected your bank, meet with your banker face to face. Talk to an officer at the bank and let them know that you're going to be traveling internationally. Some of the specific things that you will want to address with the bank are:

- safeguards for protecting your accounts and funds
- programs for managing your money
- policies and procedures for dealing with a blocked account
- logging in to your account online from a foreign IP address
- keeping the bank updated on your travel plans
- transaction fees for ATM withdrawals
- reporting lost or stolen cards
- procedures for getting replacement cards if needed
- getting a new debit and/or credit card with an expiration date that exceeds your trip plans
- cash - take some hard currency with you. US dollars, British pounds or Euros are best. Make sure you have new, fresh, crisp, unmarked, unstamped bills. Many places around the world will not accept foreign currency with even the slightest mark on it.
- national and branch contact numbers and e-mail addresses

Credit and Debit Cards

There are a few steps you need to take to facilitate the use of your credit and debit card.

- **Get two credit cards.** Get these before you quit your job. In order of importance, get a Visa first, then a MasterCard, and finally, an American Express card.

- **Get a four-digit PIN number for each card.** If you have a five-digit PIN, you must change this to a four-digit number, which is the most universally accepted worldwide. Not all countries' ATMs allow for five digits.

- **Get cards with smart chips if possible.** Much of the world is migrating to smart chip technology. If your card doesn't have one, it's not fatal, but it may make it harder to use your card in some parts of the world.

- **Investigate foreign transaction fees.** This goes for both credit card purchases and ATM withdrawals. Some banks and credit card issuers do not have them or will refund them. Others can be quite high. This can be a surprise, unbudgeted expense during your trip. Some American Express cards waive these fees. For Visa and MasterCard, it's an issuer by issuer policy.

- **Research your liabilities in case of theft.** Know before you leave what your banks require of you, what numbers to call, and how much you could be liable for in case your card gets stolen or hacked.

- **Copy and scan your cards, front and back.** E-mail them to yourself, leave a copy with a trusted friend, and perhaps take a copy with you to keep in a safe place with a copy of your passport. Also, put this information in your electronic address book.

- **Pre-paid cards and traveler's checks** Let me make this easy: do not use these on your trip. It is becoming harder and harder to find places that will accept traveler's checks. As for pre-paid cards, many (if not most) cannot be used universally overseas. I traveled with a friend recently in Colombia. Her girlfriends gave her pre-paid cards to use on her trip. All of them were denied in multiple stores and restaurants. Use them domestically, not internationally.

Wills and Trusts

For peace of mind for you and for those you're leaving behind, update your will. Do not leave behind a legal mess by not having one in place. If you don't already have a will, here's your chance to finally create one. If you have significant assets and have specific ideas for how they should be dealt with, consider creating a trust; this will simplify how your money is managed after you're gone.

Life Insurance

If you do not have a life insurance policy, you should consider getting one. When I left, I bought a term policy that would pay into the trust I had created. I bought enough coverage to make sure that my funeral would be taken care of. Anything left on top of that would go into my trust and would be dealt with according to the instructions I had outlined. As I am not a licensed insurance sales representative, I can only give you general advice such as "Do this!" Only you can determine the exact type of policy that you need.

Taxes on the Road

Be sure to meet with a tax preparer to figure out the best way to deal with filing your taxes while you're away. Depending on your return date, filing an extension could be the best way to go.

Who Takes Career Breaks? Katie:
Redefining a Sense of Self

I have never done anything in my life without extensive planning. This made leaving my job one of the hardest things about preparing for my career break. I politely gave notice at work, secured references and updated my résumé, all while wondering if I was doing the right thing. I had always identified myself by what I did for a living – lawyer, event planner, fundraiser – and that identity suddenly disappeared. I didn't know what I would do when I returned and that lack of a plan terrified me.

As I prepare to return, I am still scared but I feel like I have found direction during my travels, picking up work writing and editing while also growing my travel blog. I have accepted that some things – like a weather-delayed ferry or a difficult border crossing – are simply beyond my control. And I have learned that things have a way of working out.

Katie recently returned from her 13-month career break. She continues to write about her travels and her re-entry experience at KatieGoingGlobal.com.

Planning Where to Go on Your Career Break

This one is easy. Go wherever it is that you've been dying to go. There are no rules. The only must-do location is the one that you must do. It's the only criterion that matters.

But consider this point: this is your chance to go off your beaten path and experience some far-flung places that you might not otherwise visit. Include at least one place that you wouldn't otherwise have considered going.

Here are some budget considerations for you to keep in mind while planning your itinerary.

- Europe, North America, Japan, Australia and New Zealand are the most expensive regions of the world for travel. If you have a tight budget, spend less time there.
- South America (outside of the major cities) is very budget friendly. If you've never been, start in Mexico, Argentina and Chile. Bolivia, Ecuador and Colombia are also great budget spots.
- Asia is inexpensive as well. Again, you need to get out of the bigger cities and stay away from resort destinations. Your money will go very far in countries like Thailand, India, Vietnam, Cambodia, and China.
- Africa can be very reasonably priced depending on what you want to do. There are some attractions that are more expensive, like safaris, hiking Mount Kilimanjaro, and visiting the gorillas in Uganda or Rwanda. Big cities like Johannesburg, Cape Town and Nairobi are not very budget-friendly. Try Egypt, Tanzania, Ethiopia and Ghana to maximize your budget.
- Australia and New Zealand are not budget destinations, but there are ways to economize. Public transportation, trains, ferries, group shuttles between cities and a great selection of hostels can help you manage your expenses.
- The Middle East often gets overlooked on itineraries. Turkey should not be missed and once you get out of Istanbul, it's a bargain. Jordan, Oman and even Lebanon are increasingly popular and lower cost options.

Finally, don't forget about the weather when you're planning your trip. It goes beyond just choosing to travel in summer or winter. The extremes between rainy and dry seasons in some countries can have a real impact on your travel experience. Be sure to find out when to go and if the troublesome weather is localized or country-wide.

Traveling to countries off the beaten path like Colombia will help you stretch your budget.

Dealing with Your Health

You can never start too soon in planning for your health on the road. Insurance, vaccinations, first aid kits, special medications, and dealing with anxiety about what to do if you get sick are all part of it. Remember, you want peace of mind on the road. You can't control how your body will react to new places or new food, but you can control the mechanisms you have in place to deal with them.

Administrative Tasks

- **Talk to an insurance broker before you quit your job.** Health insurance rules are complex. It is important to have a licensed professional help you through the maze. In addition to your local brokers, there are national companies that can help you. The two most prominent are InsureMyTrip. com and SquareMouth.com. Individual companies with insurance you need for this type of trip are International Medical Group (IMG), Travel Guard, Medex.com and WorldNomads.
- **Set up a living will.** For the same reasons that you need to set up your will, you need to set up a living will to help manage your health decisions in case you can't. It will likely only be valid in your home country, but the instructions you provide will be invaluable to your loved ones. Don't leave it to chance.

Health Tasks

- **Vaccinations.** For peace of mind, visit your local travel clinic. If you need to be vaccinated for things like hepatitis, you must start early since these require multiple shots over a period of several months. If you are on the road and realize that you need a vaccine, the Red Cross has clinics around the world that offer shots at reasonable prices.
- **Get a small first aid kit.** You can get many of the basics on the road (often much cheaper than in your home country), but there may be a few things that you want to take with you, especially if you're going to non-English-speaking countries.
- **Have a final checkup.** Before you leave, have one final physical that includes standard blood tests (perhaps even an allergy test), and an eye exam.

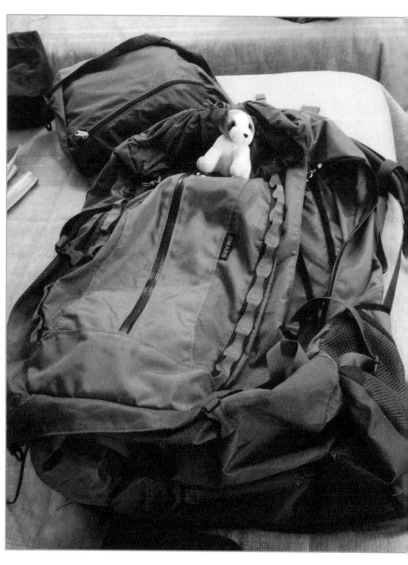

Time to downsize and figure out what you really need while you're on the road.

How to Pack for the Long Term

Want peace of mind on your trip? Pack light!

Traveling as a minimalist takes some getting used to, especially on a long-term trip. How do you decide what goes and what stays? Mostly practice. But, until then, here are a few tips to get you started:

- **Get a side-loading backpack.** It makes it easier to get your stuff in and out.
- **Use the bag wrapping services at the airport.** Backpacks are easy to get into, rifle through and close up without anyone noticing. Remember, thieves are lazy. By having a wrap around your bag, you make it more difficult for them to get into it and impossible not to notice if they did. Also, airport baggage handling systems are rough on luggage; the plastic helps keep the skid marks off your bags. Finally, if your bag has to pass through rain outside, your backpack will stay dry inside.
- **Carry on anything you can't possibly live without or that has value.** I used to think this one was obvious. Then I traveled with a good friend of mine for a couple of weeks during my career break. I was shocked at what she put in her checked luggage: important papers and even cash. Don't trust that your bags won't be opened or that the security people won't steal from you.
- **Always pack the same things in the same place inside your backpack.** For efficient packing and unpacking, have a system in which your things always go in the same place so that you know where to find them and can pack up quicker.
- **Unpack everything once in a while.** You'll be surprised at what you forgot you were carrying around, and may be able to lighten your load.
- **Check with your tour operator for their recommended packing list.** Depending on the kind of tour you take, you may need some special gear or clothing. Consider the possibility of seeking out a local second-hand store or renting the extra gear for your trip.

Here's my list of must-have items:
- iPod. Music is crucial for those long bus and plane rides.
- Microfiber towel. These are great for drying quickly.
- Small medicine kit. This is good to have in a pinch.
- Hygiene products. In particular, I take hand sanitizer, moist facial tissue and a roll of toilet paper for some countries.
- Re-sealable plastic (Ziploc) bags help keep the wet stuff wet, the dry stuff dry, and keep your easily-lost items well organized.
- Shaving cream and razor.
- Deodorant.
- Toothbrush, toothpaste, and floss.
- Sunscreen and a small container of skin lotion. Some places are really dry
- Hair brush.
- Nail file and clippers.
- Small container of hair product. It comes in handy if you get an invitation to someone's house.
- Cologne. Either a small bottle or store samples will do.
- Jeans. Some travelers hate them, but I find them very versatile when going somewhere with locals.
- One nice shirt. Again, if you get invited out, or want to go somewhere nice it will come in handy.
- Shoes. Tennis shoes, flip flops and one nice pair of black shoes will do it. If I'm going to be doing a lot of hiking, I might take hiking boots.
- Shirts for layering. Your travel fashion style will be defined by layers.
- Headlamp. If you take an iPod with you, the free Flashlight app can be an acceptable substitution.
- Locks for your bags and hostel lockers.
- Buffs (headscarves). Good for wind and sun protection, or simply adding an extra layer.
- Duct tape. It's first aid for your gear.
- Travel-size spray bottle of fabric refresher (Febreze). Things get smelly on the road!

For women, there may be a few other items that you will want to pack. I asked some of my favorite female travelers for additional suggestions.

- Jodi Ettenberg from LegalNomads.com suggests a safety whistle.
- Sarah Lee from LiveShareTravel.com suggests a pashmina and a Swiss Army knife.
- Shannon O'Donnell from ALittleAdrift.com suggests a women's menstrual cup and a sarong.
- Janice Waugh from SoloTravelerBlog.com suggests a doorstop.

Tech Tips for Your Career Break

Traveling with some type of technology is practically universal, with many considering it de rigueur. On your career break, you need to think about how connected you want to be. For some people, being near a Wi-Fi signal is critical while others would rather avoid it. If you plan on traveling with at least a few gadgets, you'll need to think about safety, protecting against breakage, and plug and voltage adaptors - not to mention packing space and enabling passwords on every device.

Here are a few tips on some popular travel gadgets and services:

- **Unlocked GSM cell phones** will keep you connected in the country you're in and will make sure that your phone will work in every country you visit. Do not get talked into using a locked phone from your current cell phone provider.
- **Local SIM cards** will get you the cheapest phone rates while traveling. Do not buy an international plan in your home country. You will almost always pay significantly more than buying a SIM card in the local country.
- **iPod Touch/Tablets/e-Readers** will provide integrated access to the web, e-mail, games, music, and books.
- **Laptops/Netbooks** will allow you to keep up with blogging, photo editing and storage, and access the Internet.
- **Boingo** will give you international Wi-Fi roaming access when a free signal is not available. Its coverage is not 100 percent, so check to see if the price

is worth it. Having Boingo does not preclude you from using free Wi-Fi services when available.

- **Blogging platforms** will give you the space to document your trip and show off your creative writing, photography and video skills.
- **Social media** will be important to help you keep in touch with your friends and family in real time, as well as other travelers you meet along the way.

Finally, many electronics now come with power plugs that can handle all types of voltage, thereby eliminating your need for a heavy voltage adaptor. Check your gadgets to see if they will work in 110W and 220/240W environments.

How to Use the Web for Planning

There are an ever-increasing number of independent travel blogs full of stories, tips, and advice that can help you during your planning stage. Some are first-person narratives full of tales of adventures and misadventures. Others offer resources with a broader perspective of informative tips and advice. Still others provide pure inspiration through travel stories, photos, and/or videos.

> ❝ *It's best to read a few bloggers on any given destination to see what the consensus is and find the voices you trust.* ❞

There are a lot of benefits to using travel blogs when you are planning a trip. The authors typically have first-hand knowledge about the destinations they write about. You can read about the travel experience without marketing hype. Bloggers also love to hear from their readers. If you have a question about something they've written or a place they've visited, write to them. Many will get back to you quickly and help you as much as they can.

There are a few things you need to keep in mind when using blogger information, however. These travelers may not have the same perspective on travel that you do. For example, while one may have loved Chile, you might not. Another might have hated the food, but you might find it delicious. It's best to read a few bloggers on any given destination to see what the consensus is and find the voices you trust.

Here are a few tips on finding travel blogs that you will love and that you will want to use in your planning.

- **Google's "Blog Search" Function.** In Google, search for a country, activity or site that interests you. When the search results come up, on the left hand side you'll see a series of tags: "Everything," "Images," "Maps," etc. Click on the "More" tag. Then, click on "Blogs." Google will give you a new set of search results from blogs around the world.
- **Blog Lists.** Google "Top Travel Blogs" and you'll see curated lists of some of the most popular and well-known travel blogs out there. Keep in mind that these lists are not perfect. First, the lists typically include only those bloggers that submitted themselves to the list. Next, the ranking criteria are mostly subjective. They are also not typically updated very frequently. The lists are updated monthly at best. Finally, these lists tend to have more professional bloggers, not current travelers.
- **Blogs' Links Pages.** Most bloggers, as a service to their readers, provide a list of other travel blogs on their site. Once you find a blog you like, navigate to its links page to see what other blogs are listed. It's a great way to get lost in the blogosphere.
- **Facebook.** Many bloggers now have Facebook pages so that they can create a community with their readers. It is also another way to get to know the bloggers that you like and keep up with their latest posts. If the blogger has a Facebook page, they will have a button on their homepage to link you directly to it.
- **Twitter.** Most bloggers use Twitter as a way to promote their latest articles and engage with other travelers, bloggers, and readers. Bloggers make use of Twitter hashtags (the # symbol) when tweeting. If you want to see who is tweeting about travel, there are a few key hashtags relevant for your career break planning.

Use these hashtags to start your research:

- #careerbreak
- #travel
- #rtw (round the world)
- #rtwnow (round the world now - current travelers)
- #rtwsoon (round the world woon - current planners)
- #photography
- **Twitter chats and events.** These are weekly and bi-weekly events hosted by bloggers with rotating topics. It's a great way to meet other travelers from around the world.
  - #TTOT (Travel Talk on Twitter), Tuesdays
  - #NUTS (Not-so Usual Therapy Session), Tuesdays
  - #TNI (Travelers' Night In), Thursdays
  - #FriFotos (Friday Photos), Fridays
- **Other social media.** Many bloggers also use Pinterest, StumbleUpon and Google+ to varying degrees. You can usually find links to all of their social media communities on their sites' homepages.
- **Local travel events.** The web also enables in-person local events. To find them, check out the following sites: Couchsurfing, Travel Massive, Meet, Plan, Go! and Meetup. If there isn't anything in your area, some of these organizations may help you start something.

Other Final Peace of Mind Details

Before you leave, don't forget these final peace of mind details.

- **Mail.** Do you want it held or forwarded to someone else? Be sure to check to see how long the post office will forward your mail (it's not forever). Be sure to change addresses as needed.
- **Bills.** Paying online is a good option if you are taking your own laptop. Never pay bills on a public computer. Be sure to log in to your accounts to make sure everything is working before you leave. Now is a good time to set up automatic payments if that's what you prefer. It's best not to use public Wi-Fi hotspots when logging in to sensitive sites.
- **Purging and storage.** For many, leaving is a good time to downsize their lives. If you want to store a few things, look around at several options. I

prefer a climate controlled unit. By using storage facilities on the outskirts of cities and towns, you can often find lower prices.

- **Pets.** By far the hardest decision I had to make was who my beagle, Max, would live with. After a lot of thought and weekend experiments with friends and family, he finally wound up with my cousin, a big dog lover and Max's former dog sitter.
- **Scans and copies.** Earlier I mentioned this in the context of your credit cards. It's good to do the same for passports, visas and anything else you think is critical to back up. E-mail a copy to yourself and save it in a special folder, leave a copy with someone trusted back home and, for some documents, carry a paper copy with you.
- **"Healthy" Flash Cards**. If you have food allergies like celiac disease, seafood or nut allergies, or even if you're simply a vegetarian, create flash cards in the foreign languages that you can use when you eat out.

Another reason to tie up all lose ends before you go: you will want to relax and enjoy exploring the fairy chimneys in the Cappadocia region of Turkey.

How to Say Goodbye

While you will only be a Skype call or a Facebook post away, leaving behind family, friends, and pets is still tough. Frankly, it's harder on those you leave behind than on you. Fun, adventure, and exotic lands are calling your name and you're mentally ready to go explore. For everyone else, it's life as usual, but without you.

There are several ways to ease the separation.

- **Throw a going away party.** The last few weeks and days before you leave will be hectic, so take the time to see your inner circle once more. You may not have time for one-on-one visits with everyone, so throw a party so that you can all see each other one last time before you go.
- **Get your family set up on Skype.** My parents were a little intimidated by Skype at first. But once we tested it out and they could see me on their computer screen, they were hooked. Years later, it's our preferred mode of communication.
- **Set up a regular call schedule.** For your closest family, have a regularly scheduled call. It gives them a bit of peace of mind that they will know where you are and can talk to you directly.
- **Set up a private Facebook group.** Chances are, most of your inner circle is on Facebook. I recommend a private group to protect yourself from future employers who may want to snoop around to see what you've been up to. A private group gives you a bit more protection than a regular group. Also, check your privacy settings on Facebook to make sure you fully understand how public or private your photos and comments will be.

inding a home for Max was the hardest decision I had to make and made it hard to say goodbye.

Just for Fun: Lessons Learned from Career Breakers

On my site, CareerBreakSecrets.com, I have an interview series called "Who's Out There Now?" I interview people who are in the midst of their break. They must have been on the road for at least three months before I will interview them. It ensures that they've had time to get into the rhythm of their trip and gain some perspective on their life and the decision that they made to travel.

After years of conducting these interviews, it is clear that there is a lot to be learned from listening to people's travel stories. Here are my picks for some of the best answers from the series. It was really hard to choose. I had to leave out so many other great answers. What really comes through in these interviews is how individualistic travel perceptions and experiences are.

I've never answered the questions myself so I'm taking the opportunity to do so now.

Best dish you've found so far
Jeff: Anything from Turkey
Best of the rest: "Uruguayan steak (we cut it with a spoon!)," HeckticTravels.com

Most exotic food eaten
Jeff: Boiled and braised camel eaten on a felucca in Egypt
Best of the rest: There were lots of good choices, but I had to select "Fermented horse milk in Kyrgyzstan," TrekkingThePlanet.net

Most breathtaking moment
Jeff: Hiking Torres del Paine in Patagonia in Chile
Best of the rest: "Watching the great wildebeest migration in Kenya," LuggageInHand.com

Biggest disappointment
Jeff: Egypt
Best of the rest: "The food in South America," ThinkingNomads.com
Honorable Mention: "Couldn't say. A disappointing day out on the road is still better than a great day in a cubicle." Trans-Americas.com

Most memorable place
Jeff: Patagonia
Best of the rest: "Audrey: Republic of Georgia. Dan: Kyrgyzstan,"
UncorneredMarket.com

Most memorable person
Jeff: Gloria, my homestay mom in Quito, Ecuador
Best of the rest: "I got to dance with the president of Ireland, and had a great
chat with her," FluentinThreeMonths.com

My most breathtaking moment was getting to know the Torres Del Paine Park in the
Chilean Patagonia.

Best thing to have on a long bus ride
Jeff: Snacks, water, and a fully charged iPod
Best of the rest: There is a lot of consensus on this question. It boils down to patience, entertainment (iPods and Kindles) and something to keep you warm.

Worst thing to have on a long bus ride
Jeff: Stomach issues
Best of the rest: Again, there's a lot of agreement. Stomach issues topped the list. But the best answer here was, "A 65-year-old Turkish seatmate trying to convince you to become his 4th wife on a 12-hour overnight bus to Istanbul," AngieAway.com

Best thing you packed
Jeff: My iPod
Best of the rest: "My diva cup," ALittleAdrift.com

Worst thing you packed
Jeff: Skis. Honestly, what was I thinking?
Best of the rest: There are plenty of great responses here, but I had to choose, "Make-up...and condoms come a close second – I think it was wishful thinking!" Ottsworld.com

Funniest travel habit you have
Jeff: I am addicted to sparkling water. I seek it out wherever I am.
Best of the rest: "I travel with my stuffed animals and space ice cream," RunawayJuno.com

Place you wish you could have stayed longer
Jeff: Turkey
Best of the rest: There were too many diverse places to choose from, so I'm choosing this answer which sums up the sentiment of many of the interviews: "Everywhere," LegalNomads.com

MAKING THE MOST OF YOUR TRIP

*Life is a great big canvas
and you should throw all the
paint you can on it*

Danny Kaye

I spent a month in Bariloche, Argentina accomplishing one of my goals: learning to ski.

Learning to Let Go on the Road

"OK Jeff, voy a quitarte los bastones."

After a day and a half of struggling to turn myself without falling on the slopes outside Bariloche, Argentina, my ski instructor told me he was going to take my poles away. Gulp. My anxiety shot up. To my left, four five-year-olds were skiing downhill without poles as if it were natural, no big deal. But, at the age of thirty-seven, skiing was anything but effortless.

The snow-white, forested mountains overlooking the placid Lake Nahuel Huapi were stunning, but they didn't relax me. Pablo faced me, stuck his crossed arms out, and I held on for dear life as we made our way down the mountain. By the time we arrived at the bottom of the run, I had relaxed, learned to guide myself by my hips, and finally conquered a critical milestone in learning to ski. I was on my way to achieving one of the goals of my trip. I was also learning how to live in the moment again.

Adjusting to a "Free" Life

No phone calls, over-scheduled agendas, late night meetings, fire-drills, or days and nights away from your family and friends. Now you have it: complete freedom. What are you going to do with it? By the time you get here, you probably already have some idea and you may have even gone into over-planning craziness. Now, I want you to do three things:

STOP.

BREATHE.

THINK.

This is your time. It's your moment. And it can be oddly unsettling. I remember my first week off the job. No phones, no e-mails, no crazy schedules. The house was quiet. Inexplicably, my mind went right back to the office. I started thinking about the projects I had left, and I wondered how my colleagues were. Here I was, free to go off and travel, and what was I thinking about? Work. It was as if I was suffering from some sort of weird work-induced Stockholm Syndrome.

Thank God that passed!

I think what I really missed was the social aspect of work. My job had become such a dominant part of my life that, sadly, many of my social needs were met there.

My life started filling up with other activities before I left for my trip. The gym figured prominently in my daily regimen as I sought to lose a good deal of the weight that I had gained over the years. My social life filled up again. And, of course, just dealing with the details of sorting my life kept me busy.

Dealing with the freedom to do what you want to do isn't as easy as it sounds. Paradoxically, working crazy hours can make us lazy. We allow our schedules to be dominated by the jumps from one work deadline to the next. Our personal lives supplement the remaining time we have. So, when those deadlines are gone, a void of activity appears and we're temporarily left wondering what to do.

> 66 *They have been in control of their decisions, not pushed externally to achieve, but driven internally to pursue their passions and dreams.* 99

During your career break, you will have a lot of downtime and alone time. If you're not comfortable being by yourself, you will have no choice but to become so. Long airplane and bus rides, and exploring countries where you don't speak the language, create the solitude. It's freeing, it's isolating, but it is not necessarily lonely. It's not unusual for career breakers to pass a day or two in which they speak to hardly anyone.

Over time, you get used to this ultimate freedom and you become accustomed to taking charge of your life once again. Whether you are so inclined or not, travel forces you to be self-starting, self-motivating, or simply reinforces those qualities that you already possess. If you are taking a career break, there's probably already a touch of that within you. But those tendencies will become more pronounced, more visible, over time.

It's one of the reasons why career breakers return with so much confidence. They've had to live life deliberately. They have been in control of their decisions, not pushed externally to achieve, but driven internally to pursue their passions and dreams.

Where will your new free life take you?

Who Takes Career Breaks? Bethany & Ted:
Sharing Skills, Gaining Experience

Ted is a social worker, and I am a landscape architect. I wished to make time for an extended trip around the world after studying abroad in New Zealand. Eight years later, Ted and I made good on the dream, stepping away from our careers to travel for thirteen months.

While exploring new continents and cultures, we embrace opportunities to add to our skill sets and shape sensitive perspectives in our personal and professional lives. Ted interviewed the former head of social services for La Paz, Bolivia, learning inspiring stories to apply to his future work. I volunteered my site planning skills in exchange for accommodation, saving money on the road and adding international projects to my professional portfolio.

We travel with the confidence that developing deeper understandings of the people, groups, and ecosystems of the world will complement our long-term career tracks.

Bethany and Ted pressed the reset button on work and life and are currently on their career break, sharing their photos and stories at twoOregonians.com

Three Things that Career Breakers Do

I've known and talked to hundreds of career breakers from all over the world. No matter the catalyst, the reason or goal of the break, we all want to make our time count. Sure, career breakers see the typical tourist sites. I even became a fan of the double-decker, hop on-hop off buses during my career break. But beyond that, we actively look to do something that's special to us. We may not feel the need to change the world, but we are looking to transition to the next phase of our lives, to push ourselves, to experience something new, real, and authentic.

1. Volunteer and Give Back

One of the most popular things for career breakers to do is to give back. Rather than giving an hour or a day, they take the opportunity to dedicate a few weeks, or, in some cases, months to an organization. Others even choose several organizations as they volunteer around the world.

There are so many options available. Choosing an organization and a project are big decisions. Shannon O'Donnell covers this topic quite extensively in *The Volunteer Traveler's Handbook*. I recommend it for anyone who wants to include volunteering in their career break.

In the meantime, here are a few tips to find the right experience for you:

- Think about the skills you have to offer. As someone with a career, you have skills that organizations can use.
- Match your skills to the needs of the organizations that you are interested in working with.
- Ask lots of questions and talk to former volunteers to find out what the experience is like.

At the end of your time, not only will you have given back, you'll have gained some great experience to add to your résumé.

2. See the World in Cool Ways

A career break trip allows you to see the world in different ways. It allows you to stop rushing and start learning about the culture, the landscape, and the people. Often, with a little extra online research or talking to locals, you can discover more fulfilling transportation options that can add extra depth to your experience.

Why fly to southern Chile when you can take a four-day ferry along the southern Patagonian coast? Why take a train in Spain when you can walk across it? Why take a bus between cities in New Zealand when you can bike across the country? You'll meet people you never would have met otherwise, see parts of the country that are not well-traveled, and experience aspects of the local culture that might otherwise have eluded you.

Here are a few cool things you can do on each continent.
- North America: Hike the Appalachian Trail, take a cross-country road trip.
- South America: Conquer some of the great hikes of the world including Machu Picchu, The Lost City, El Cocuy, Torres Del Paine, El Chaltén or Aconcagua. Ferry the Amazon from Colombia to the Atlantic Brazilian Coast or down the Patagonian coast in Chile.
- Asia: Hike the Lycian Way in Turkey, take the Trans-Siberian rail, motorbike across Vietnam or tackle the Annapurna Circuit in Nepal.
- Africa: Bike from Cairo to Cape Town or hike Kilimanjaro.
- Oceania: Bike across New Zealand, sail through the Pacific islands, or rent a van and camp throughout the Australian Outback.
- Europe: Hike the Camino de Santiago, or take the trains from east to west, north to south.
- Antarctica: Kayak along the coast and include a stop in the Falklands and South Georgia Islands.

3. Learn Something New
A career break is the perfect time to focus on that hobby you've been neglecting, or conquer a goal you've set for yourself. In my case, I studied Spanish to achieve fluency, passing the DELE (Diplomas of Spanish as a Foreign Language) exam at the Superior level. I also learned to ski. I met a man who went paragliding around the world. Language, cooking, sailing, photography, writing, basket weaving - what is it that you've always wanted to do but never seemed to have the time for? A career break is a great time to focus on those passions and mix them in with your travel.

Here are a few ideas for filling your time around the world:

- language classes to pick up Spanish, Chinese or Zulu
- cooking classes in some of the world's great culinary destinations like Thailand, France, Spain, India
- dancing classes like salsa in Colombia, or tango in Argentina
- photography, writing or video production courses
- diving instruction so you can explore some of the best dive sites in the world
- learn a new instrument, music, and songs through the local cultures
- winery tours, learning the art of coffee cultivation, discovering how chocolate is produced - take your hobby to the next level, whatever it may be.

Hiking Waynapicchu gives you a birds-eye view of Machu Picchu... if you get an early start.

Who Takes Career Breaks? Toby & David:
Connecting, Teaching, Learning

We always knew our career break would be a long one—close to a year in length. But as we were planning, it just seemed overly indulgent to make an eleven-month itinerary completely self-serving. So we created the Global Encounter Experience: a way to share our adventure with elementary school children around the world.

Our travel would serve as a teaching medium to share experiences, culture, and world history. Based on America's position on the globe, we're not exposed to a wide variety of cultures and people. Opportunities to learn life lessons by experiencing and valuing other customs and ways of life are limited.

Through our online videos and curriculum, Global Encounter illustrates for students that the impossible is actually quite achievable. By confounding the status quo through our year-long trip around the world, we hope to teach and challenge students to overcome the hurdles to success in their own lives.

David and Toby are currently on their career break, traveling, volunteering, and educating along the way. Follow their journey at Global-Encounter.com

Dealing with Loneliness

On May 7th I headed off to Spanish class in Quito, Ecuador. It was my birthday. Knowing that I wouldn't be surrounded by family and friends, I planned for a low-key day and went about my business. During the first school break, all of the students gathered in the quad, and out came a birthday cake. Over the next ten minutes, "Happy Birthday" was sung to me in English, Spanish, Chinese, and German. It was an unexpected surprise. I admit that my mental toughness melted. I laughed as it became apparent that the "Happy Birthday" melody is the same the world over. I may have been separated from my inner circle, but I was hardly alone or lonely.

The thought of going to dinner or to a movie alone is beyond the pale for many people. So suggesting that they go traveling alone is practically unimaginable. But people with intense wanderlust are no longer letting it stop them. Long-term travelers develop various ways of coping with solo travel to thrive on the road.

- **Get to know other travelers at your hostel.** Hostels are great places to meet people. All you have to do is go camp out in the common areas and before you know it, you'll be talking to others.
- **Use technology to stay connected to those back home.** You will have great stories to tell from the road and people want to hear from you. So, whether you use Facebook, simple e-mail, a blog, Skype or Google Voice, you will have lots of ways to stay in touch.
- **Get an unlocked GSM cell phone.** If you plan to use a cell phone on your trip, you need to get an unlocked phone so that it will work in all countries using local SIM cards.
- **Start in a country where you speak the local language.** To minimize culture shock when career breakers first start traveling, I've known several people who started in countries where their native tongue is spoken.
- **Start with a local tour.** Traveling in a small group gives you instant, like-minded travel companions. Small group tours are my preference.
- **Treat yourself to comfort food.** Sometimes you just need a taste of something familiar.

Travel Friendships

"Jeff. JEEEEFF!"

I had just passed through customs in Buenos Aires and was boarding the ferry to head to Uruguay for a week. Who the hell could be calling my name here? I turned around, perplexed, then smiled. I couldn't believe my eyes.

Melanie and Fabian, a Dutch couple I had met on my tour of the Galapagos Islands in Ecuador five months prior, were on the same boat. It was then that I realized that the backpacking circuit on the huge continent of South America was a lot smaller than I had thought. We caught up on our travels over coffee and it was like no time had passed.

We intended to get together in Punta del Este a few days after the ferry crossing. Unfortunately, their plans changed and we didn't meet up again until a year later when I went to visit them in Amsterdam. In fact, I interviewed them for my website, stayed in their house and got to meet their new baby son. We still keep in touch from time to time. Do I know them well? No. But we have a special connection and friendship that will last a lifetime.

Befriending other travelers is a unique experience. No matter where you are from, your common interest in the destination brought you to the same place - and that's a great starting point. Your place in the social order is not based on your career, where you live or where you went to school. In that moment, the only thing that matters is your shared interest and desire to explore and get to know the destination.

That's not to say that conflicts won't arise. Differences in budgets, travel styles, sleeping habits, and people's own comfort levels can affect your relationships. You may only spend an afternoon, a day or a few days with them. From then on, you're all heading off to different destinations. Then the cycle begins again.

There is something special about travel friendships, even if they only last a day. They are intense. Unencumbered by personal history or the social constraints of life at home, travelers tend to bare their souls to each other. I've had more than one conversation in which one of us said, "Even people back home don't know this about me."

> 66 *The only questions you need to ask to start meeting people are, "What do you recommend seeing around here?" or "What did you see today?"* 99

There's a freedom that you feel when you are on the road. It's raw. It's honest. Maybe it's the anonymity you experience. Perhaps it's a kinship you feel with other people who are as passionate as you are about travel discovery. And often, it's brief. They say that friendships and relationships are for a reason, a season or a lifetime. You will find a mix of all three on your career break.

When you're just getting started, remember this. The only questions you need to ask to start meeting people are, "What do you recommend seeing around here?" or "What did you see today?" Travelers love to talk about their travels, and everyone has an opinion about "the best thing to do." So break the ice with these questions and let the conversation flow.

You'll meet people everywhere, even on a ferry off the southern Chilean Patagonian coast.

Who Takes Career Breaks? Paul:
Finding Love Unexpectedly

I took my career break in 2007. I'd been working in the same job in the UK for around ten years and was planning to spend some time in South America between posts. To test the waters, I went to Chile for five weeks. I figured I would learn some Spanish, travel around a bit, meet some new people, head back to England, and think about returning.

My life changed unexpectedly during a night out with students from the language school where I was studying. I was in a nightclub when suddenly a gorgeous girl said hello to me. She explained that she was trying to get away from a strange man who was talking to her. "A case of out of the frying pan and into the fire," I thought, but we started talking and got on great right away. We met up again a couple of days later and started going out together. We stayed in contact every day after I returned to England. I knew Ale was the one, so I returned to Chile later in the year. We moved in together and subsequently got married there in 2010.

Paul and his wife have moved to London where Paul found a job using the Spanish fluency he gained from studying and living in Chile.

Staying Safe on the Road

There are three aspects to safety and security on the road: your personal safety, the security of your possessions, and your digital security. Over time, managing your safety will become second nature. If you're not already street smart, you will be after your career break.

Personal Safety

- **Register your trip with your embassy.** The chances that your embassy will have to contact you are remote, but registering with them will streamline communications in the event that something happens. Many embassies have online forms you can fill out.
- **Rely on the locals and other travelers to get the real scoop.** If someone wants to give you advice about the safety of a place, ask if they've been there recently. You'll be surprised at how many haven't. Also, many places that have a tinge of danger to their reputation either aren't dangerous, have it localized to places where you wouldn't go anyway, or have special "rules" to minimize your risk.
- **Take only what you need for the day.** There is no need to pack your entire life when you go out exploring for the day. Don't take your passport (a copy will usually be fine), wallet or any credit or debit cards that you're not going to use. Keep your daypack light.
- **Safety in numbers.** If the idea of throwing yourself out into the world is still a little daunting, then join up with a small group tour operator when you first arrive to a new country. It will give you time to adjust to your new surroundings.
- **Make friends at your hostel.** Go to the common area and strike up a conversation with someone at your hostel. They will probably appreciate making a new friend to hang out with too.
- **Nighttime safety.** Security situations can vary greatly between the day and night. Always find out if you need to get around differently at night than you do during the day.
- **Whistle while you walk.** Jodi Ettenberg, founder of LegalNomads.com and author of *The Food Traveler's Handbook*, swears by having a safety whistle on you at all times.

Security of Your Goods and Information

- **Address prevention before you leave.** Allow me to make one final reminder. Don't leave without making photocopies of all of your key items. Keep one copy with you, scan one copy, and e-mail it to yourself so you can print it on the road, and as extra backup, leave a copy with a trusted family member or friend back home.
- **Put it here, not there.** Front pockets and bras are best. Some people swear by money belts. I don't. Back pockets and outer backpack compartments are the worst option.
- **Locks.** Consider locking the zippers on your backpack. I've seen a few travelers do this to give them peace of mind while walking around.
- **Keep your electronics hidden.** The price of these gadgets in many countries makes them highly desired by thieves. Don't pull them out when you are walking around on the street.
- **Get black earbuds.** White headphones are an unmistakable marker of an iPod. Replace them with black ones and place the cord underneath your shirt so it is harder to notice that you are listening to your favorite songs while walking down the street or sitting on the bus.
- **Take visual cues from the locals.** How people actually walk around is as instructive as a conversation with them. Are people walking around flashing their goods? Are people using small bags easily nestled against their bodies?

Digital Security

- **Banking.** Don't do your online banking at public kiosks or Internet cafes. Access these accounts on a device and Internet connection that you know are secure. The bank may not allow access from a computer without its digital cookie. A public computer may not have adequate browser security to protect your most personal financial data.
- **Log out.** I have been in more than one Internet cafe in which the person before me did not log out of their e-mail, instant messenger or Facebook account. These people were lucky - I just logged them out. Don't give ne'er-do-wells a chance to get into your business.
- **Unsecured Wi-Fi networks.** While it's becoming rarer, occasionally you'll find an unsecured Wi-Fi signal allowing you to connect to the web.

Be careful. Sometimes these are simply traps to steal people's passwords and digital identities. Make sure you trust the source of the signal before using it.

- **Password protect all your devices.** No matter what gadgets you carry, be sure to enable password protection. Make sure the password is not something obvious like "1234." Many devices now allow for all the data to be erased automatically after a number of unsuccessful log-in attempts.
- **Consider a Virtual Private Network (VPN).** These are no longer just for corporations and can provide an added layer of security for your Internet transactions.

Stay alert and watch out for creepy crawlies and other not-so-obvious hazards.

Who Takes Career Breaks? Larissa & Michael: *Breaking Before Retirement*

After turning fifty, we quit our jobs and ditched our possessions to travel around the world for a year. Our goal was also to feel like we were living in, not just passing through, each destination.

Rather than staying at hotels, we've rented places in every country so that we can cook for ourselves, shop in neighborhood markets, meet people well off the tourist path, and live as much as possible like locals.

In the bush country of Australia, a neighboring rancher took us out at dusk for an impromptu kangaroo-viewing safari on his 3,000-acre cattle station. As his pickup truck bounced around the rugged terrain in search of the elusive marsupials, we realized that this was an experience we wouldn't have had at a hotel.

Larissa and Michael are currently on their career break. They are writing about their journey for the Philadelphia Inquirer and on their blog www.ChangesInLongitude.com

Money Management Tips on the Road

Beyond staying safe, money management is one of the top concerns you'll have while traveling. Acquiring local currency when you arrive in a new country, getting rid of it when you leave, carrying just enough (but no more) cash to get through the day, and wondering if there is even an ATM where you're going are just a few of the challenges you'll face. Here are a few tips and tricks that I have learned along the way to help give you peace of mind.

Administrative Tasks

- **Communicate with your bank.** Start by letting your banks know where you're going. It is important that all banks at which you have credit or debit card accounts are aware that you will be away and that they should expect constant overseas activity. You don't want any surprises while traveling. Banks have sophisticated fraud systems. If you haven't been traveling, then suddenly overseas charges start showing up, your account may be flagged. Even after traveling for a year, my credit card account was flagged when I bought a new camera. Once I contacted the bank, everything was fine again. It's good that they are watching but you don't want every transaction held up.
- **Set up a power of attorney with someone back home.** Depending on your situation, it could be helpful to have a trusted person back home able to access your banking information and perform transactions for you. Check with your bank to find out what documentation and signatures need to be on file.

Practical Travel Tips

- **Use ATMs for cash.** You tend to get the best exchange rate via the bank even though banks charge withdrawal fees. Some banks will waive or refund those fees. Do your homework before you go and move your account as needed. If you have to use a currency exchange service (it happens), then find one away from the airport to get the best rate. Also, withdrawing the maximum amount that you're comfortable carrying around will minimize fees.

- **Some additional advice about ATMs:**
  - Exercise caution at the ATM at all times. Find one that's guarded when possible.
  - If you don't have a four-digit ATM PIN, get one before you leave. Four-digit pins, not five, are the most universally accepted worldwide.
  - Pay attention to cash withdrawal limits. Some countries have a limit on how much money you can get per transaction, but you can often perform a second withdrawal if you need more.
- **Always have a backup plan.** Sometimes the credit card machine doesn't work. Sometimes the ATM is out of money. Sometimes the business says it takes credit cards, but it doesn't. Have multiple options available to minimize hassles.
- **Pay in the local currency.** You will get the best price using local currencies. While there are a couple of exceptions to this rule, most notably Myanmar and Cambodia, don't make the locals work to change your currency to theirs. It will cost you.
- **Know that cash is king in most of the world.** Outside of western countries, cash is not only preferred but is also often the only way to pay.

Budget Stretchers While on the Road

For a lot of people, managing their budget on the road is a game. How much can I get for how little? But staying on track doesn't have to mean bottom-of-the-barrel travel. There are a few tricks that you can use to get more for your money while you're on the road, and forge a better connection to the country and its people at the same time.

Go to a few countries and fewer continents. The term "Round-The-World Trip" is often used as a synonym for a career break trip, but there's no rule that says you have to go around the world. Stay in one region and travel to contiguous countries overland to save money on trans-oceanic airfare.

Rent an apartment. Often for the price of a night in a hostel, you can get a studio, or even a one-bedroom apartment. It allows you a place to nest, a

Local cooking classes like the one I took in India are not only fun, but will help you eat cheaply and like a local while you're on the road.

kitchen to cook for yourself, and a chance to see a side of the city or town you might not have seen otherwise.

Shop at the local markets. Grocery stores are fine, but a local vegetable and fruit market is a great place to get your ingredients just like the locals.

Stay in neighborhoods outside the tourist zones. Not only are room prices cheaper, but so is everything else: food, Internet cafes, transportation. Locals use those resources and the prices will reflect that.

Take the night bus or night train. Kill two birds with one stone by getting to your next destination and having a place to lay your head for the night. Not all are super comfortable, and some can be cold. But, you can rest a bit once you arrive at your destination if you need to.

Don't use money exchange services. Sometimes you can't avoid doing so, but it's much cheaper to use an ATM to get local currency.

Rent a car with a group. Road trips are great, but the cost of renting a car just for you may often be outside your budget. Find others in your hostel who are up for exploring by car and you can have a great day out.

Use local buses and trains. Even though taxis can be cheap in many foreign countries, the local transportation will be even cheaper. This is a great way to save money for other adventures.

Take advantage of Skype and Google Voice. You don't need to make long distance calls when there are great free services like these available.

Have patience and flexibility with your schedule. When I was in Ecuador, I was able to save enough money on my trip to the Galapagos Islands to pay for a side trip to the Amazon because I was willing to wait an extra week. I also bought a discounted trip to Easter Island when I was in Chile because I could shift my schedule to leave almost immediately. If you have patience and flexibility with your schedule, you can sometimes save a bundle. This is another reason not to over-plan your itinerary.

Eat street food. In many countries, some of the best food is also the cheapest and most widely accessible. Find busy stalls and have a good look to see how it's being made. If you're near a university, there's probably a good option around. Find a student and ask.

The Value of Learning the Local Language

Zoe and I arrived to the small fishing village of Eçeabet in the late afternoon. It would be our jumping-off point to see Gallipoli and Troy over the next couple of days. It was too early for dinner so we headed over to the small dock where the fishermen were returning as the sun began to set.

The cats were lined up waiting for any scraps to be thrown their way. Across from the docks, I saw a man with his back to us who was facing the ocean, perched on some boulders. I wanted to take a photo. He finally looked over at us and I raised my camera and smiled. He nodded his head and turned his back to us again. After snapping the pictures, I yelled at him, "Two sugars and a dream. Two sugars and a dream."

Even after three weeks in Turkey, "Two sugars and a dream" or "teşekkür ederim," was the closest I could get to saying "thank you" in Turkish. It wasn't that close, but good enough to let people know that I knew what thank you was, and that I was making an effort. It almost always brought a smile from even the most stoic faces.

The fisherman turned back towards us, nodded and smiled without letting his cigarette fall out of his mouth. My pronunciation of "thank you" was hardly perfect, but he knew I was trying and was appreciative.

There is no separating language from cultural identity. The simple act of trying to say a few words in the local language will set you apart from the vast majority of travelers. It demonstrates respect and gives you a chance to make a local connection, even if it's brief.

Hello. Goodbye. Please. Thank you. These are the obvious starting points. If a local takes you under their wing, you can learn more. You will be remembered and perhaps positively shape the view they have of people from your country.

Who Takes Career Breaks? Tony & Meg:
A Chance to Get More out of Life

Back home, we had conventionally great jobs as a business management consultant and a commercial banker. We were passionate about each other, but couldn't say the same about our careers.

Our honeymoon in 2010 put everything into perspective. We vacationed in the Virgin Islands where we met several people who made their living volunteering (or working for pennies) on yachts around the world.

We envied their happiness and immediately got the itch to travel and explore our passions.

For us, a life filled with variety, potential, and new opportunities provides an exponentially greater amount of happiness than the traditional path. We have climbed Machu Picchu in torrential rain, worked on a farm in Tuscany, and had our marriage survive a tandem biking attempt while wine tasting in Argentina. Now we are trying to start a business so that we can turn these adventures of a lifetime into a lifetime of adventures.

Using their career break as a hopeful springboard into a new life, Meg and Tony are documenting their travels around the world and their attempts at starting a business at LandingStanding.com.

Should You Work During Your Career Break?

Frankly, my inclination is to say "NO!" The whole idea behind a career break is to take a break from your career. You just left your job to go see the world, to pursue your personal passions. Why on earth would you want to get a job?

In some cases I concede that there are good reasons to work while on your trip. Even if one of the reasons is financial, as with many other aspects of your career break, think about what you can get out of the experience.

- **It will help finance your trip.** Sometimes, once you get out on the road, you want to stay a little bit longer. Finding a part-time job can help supplement your savings and make them go further. Be aware that pay scales vary widely in the world and you may make significantly less than you would at home for the same type of job.
- **You want international experience.** Lisa, a three-time Emmy award-winning producer from Chicago and editor of LLWorldTour.com, found a variety of positions while traveling. "I found jobs of all types while traveling, from a barista in Melbourne to a public relations advisor in Spain to a research assistant at the University of Cologne. I did some freelance proofreading for Turkey's largest media group (since their TV programming work is all in Turkish, it was hard to find much more work). I did interview with several Turkish TV networks and production companies and in every case, they were eager to meet someone from the professional US television market, and my résumé was more impressive to them than I gave myself credit for. Beyond location work, I worked online as a location-independent entrepreneur: writing, blogging, photographing, and consulting."
- **You want to try out a new career.** A former consulting buddy of mine, Jeremy, had always wanted to go from amateur photographer to pro. On his career break through Asia, he focused on his craft, even setting up his own site to sell his photos. He noted, "It didn't work out for me, unfortunately. The photography business was much harder to break into than I realized. But I loved all of the time that I spent perfecting my skills. I didn't want to be sixty years old and think that I had never taken a risk or a chance on something. Even though I returned to corporate life, I do

not regret having experimented with a new career. Now I don't have to live with the 'what ifs' in my mind."

- **You are considering becoming an expat.** I met Eva in Patagonia. We were on the same ferry to Puerto Natales, Chile and then we traveled through Torres Del Paine together with a few other travelers. A veterinarian from Holland, she had always dreamed of moving to Argentina. While she found a few odd jobs with local vets, she learned that it would take longer than she was willing to invest to get her license and start her own business. In the meantime, she was able to connect with the people and culture of Argentina.

RE-ENTRY

*Once you have traveled, the voyage never ends,
but is played out over and over again in the
quietest chambers. The mind can never
break off from the journey.*

Pat Conroy

Places that you never knew existed will stay with you after your career break. For me, one of those places is Villa de Leyva, Colombia.

Adjusting to Life Back Home

"You mean I have to go back?"

Well, you may not go back to the life you left, but most people are not looking to become permanent nomads. Leaving the road is a welcome change for some, but for many others, it's a necessary evil. You've just had, quite possibly, the most exciting and fulfilling time of your life. And when you get back, you will be excited to reconnect with your family and friends and tell them all about your adventures.

It's important to keep in mind that just as your life has gone on, so has everyone else's. Maybe they didn't travel around the world like you, but they've had changes to their relationships, new births, career changes, and their own travel adventures.

Have realistic expectations about how people will respond to you and your travels. Remember that these experiences happened to you, not to them. Yes, they will be interested and excited for you, but only to a point. It's unrealistic for them to have the same excitement or attention span that you have for sharing your travel tales.

Quick Reminder about Planning for Re-entry

Once you get back, you will be tackling the nuts and bolts of getting your life at home started again: looking for a job, maybe looking for a place to live, etc. The best way to start managing your life again is to plan for re-entry before you leave. Here is a quick reminder of some tips I mentioned earlier in previous sections.

- **Budget for your re-entry.** Think back to when you set your budget. Take my advice for planning to have funds set aside while you get started again. My best advice is to be conservative and plan to have a daily budget as close as possible to what you needed before you left. You probably have learned how to be more budget conscious while you were away, but it's best to have that cushion.

- **Update your résumé with your experience to date.** As I said earlier, write all those details down about your accomplishments while they are still fresh in your mind. After a few months on the road, you may have forgotten some key ones.
- **Keep in touch with your network while traveling.** Many people will be excited to follow along with you on your trip and feel a little voyeuristic about keeping up with you. Stay in touch to keep the lines of communication open. That way when you get back, it will be a natural evolution of the relationship.

Who Takes Career Breaks? Jason & Aracely: *Getting Restarted in Corporate*

After one year of traveling around the world, we re-entered corporate life. How did we do it? The truth is, it's not easy. We each have our daydreaming sessions where we picture ourselves somewhere else in the world, free of stress, free of consumerism, and free in spirit.

The reality, however, is that we are back working in the United States, but with our priorities in order. Currently, we are where we want to be in life. As long as you continue to set goals, prioritize them, and make sure that you can find happiness, you will adjust. It will never be easy, but life rarely is. Continue to evaluate and realize that it's okay to change desires, goals, and priorities along the way.

Jason and Aracely still blog about travel on 2Backpackers.com

Getting Started Again

You've kept up with everyone, you took care of all the details before you left, and now you're back. What now? The process isn't all that different than when you were out looking for that first job. This time you have several advantages you didn't have then: you have a network in place, a résumé full of great experience, and you're a little more interesting after having taken a big trip. Now it's time to start networking. Here are a few tips:

- **Update your résumé with your career break.** Here's where having been active will be a bonus for you. Every potential employer is going to want you to explain your time away anyway. You don't need to hide from your break, nor should you. Did you volunteer? Did you study? Did you work? Talk about your experience on your résumé in terms that show your employer that you broadened and/or deepened your skill set.
- **Get in touch with your professional network.** Some of your former work colleagues are going to want to hear about your trip. Invite them out to lunch or for a coffee. Make the conversation a two-way street. Do not dominate it with all the details of your trip. Be sure to ask them what is new with them. Listening while reconnecting may uncover a new opportunity for you.
- **Reach out to your college networks.** If you haven't been involved with your local alumni group, now is the perfect time to join. Having an alma mater in common is a great starting point to meet new people and broaden your network.
- **Do some public speaking.** Many libraries, small civic groups, and charitable organizations invite speakers in from time to time. To them, you are a brave world traveler living in their community. You've got great stories to tell. It's an unconventional way to get yourself out in front of a group of strangers who just might need your savvy skills, or know someone who does.
- **Update your social networks.** (Facebook, LinkedIn, etc.) Let everyone know that you're back and looking to find a job. Also, check your Facebook postings to make sure there's nothing that could disqualify you from a job.

- **Stay connected to the travel community.** You're probably going to miss the road and interacting with other travelers. There's no reason that you have to let it all go. Use the same networks that you used on the road and before you left.

Finally, there is a great organization in the US and the UK called *iRelaunch*. Founded by Carol Fishman Cohen and Vivian Steir Rabin, iRelaunch helps people who have been out of work for a while on career breaks, whether they were family or travel related. They have a wide network of companies that are open to hiring people just like you. They also run several workshops throughout the year. They are not a recruiting firm. Rather, they help you positively position yourself and your career break for prospective employers.

Who Takes Career Breaks? Bryan & Laurie:
Restarting as Entrepreneurs

Before we left for our trip we had hit some professional stumbling blocks and were scrambling to figure out what to do with our lives. We left our cubicles feeling a little disheartened by office life and we wanted to find creative ways to redevelop our careers. While we were on the road we saw many different life paths.

We met people working as guides in the Himalayas, shopkeepers in India, and social workers in Ethiopia. Many people we met had used their surroundings, their interests, and their environment to create a life for themselves. There were entrepreneurs from every walk of life. By seeing how so many people could take control and make it work, we gained confidence that with our skills and experience we could create a business in BudgetYourTrip.com that would not only help us financially to reach our goals, but also professionally and recreationally.

Bryan and Laurie have taken several career breaks which have taken them around the world. They currently run the travel site BudgetYourTrip.com.

Tips for Positioning Your Career Break

Now that you're back and are a seasoned world traveler, it's time to package what you learned and what you did for your résumé. The dreaded résumé gap will be there so address it directly and with confidence. You can't control how an employer or recruiter will view it initially, but you can influence how they perceive it eventually. Here's how and what to highlight.

- **Don't hide from it.** This break is now a part of who you are, the skills you have, and the experience you can bring to the employer. Highlight the active parts of the break to show how much of a "take charge" self-starter you really are.
- **Highlight any volunteer experience.** If you spent time volunteering, treat that experience like any work experience. What were your responsibilities, what did you accomplish and what is its relevance to the position you're applying for?
- **Identify new and improved creative skills.** Did you write, photograph, or make videos of your trip? Even if these skills are only tangentially related to the position, it still shows your curiosity and drive to improve your skill set. Include a small portfolio of your work to show off.
- **Showcase interviews with other bloggers and media.** Assuming you don't have anything disqualifying in your interviews, show your employers that your trip was so amazing that the media took notice.
- **Highlight work experience.** If you worked on your career break, be sure to highlight that. Again, tell them what your responsibilities were, what you achieved, and how it is relevant to the position you're applying for.
- **Identify other relevant soft skills.** Taking a career break teaches you a lot about yourself. It has probably made you a stronger person. Don't be afraid to share a relevant anecdote of how you got out of a sticky situation on the road to illustrate what type of soft skills you have to bring to the job.

You can't plan fashion like this, but you can plan for a successful exit, trip and re-entry.

A Final Word

I could not have imagined the life that I found while traveling on my career break. I see the world differently now. Did I fundamentally change and become a completely new person? No. But I did fill in many of the gaps I saw in my life from having been so career-focused.

I met people I would never have met, some of whom are my friends to this day. I tried things I wouldn't have otherwise. I unwound and let go. I got a truer sense of what my real boundaries were. I am more relaxed, more confident, and more patient. I don't worry as much about things that are out of my control.

After spending almost two years traveling the world, having to figure out where to eat, where to sleep, how to get around, often in a language that wasn't my own, I feel like I can accomplish anything I set my mind to.

A career break is a time in your life when you focus on you, your passions, and your interests. It's an active phase in your life when you take the energy, focus and drive that you've been putting into your career, and invest it in YOU! It's an opportunity for you to do amazing things.

Career paths are changing. The power to control our lives is in our hands. Remember *The 3% Perspective*? A global view of the world and experience living in it is valued in a way it never has been before. The only permission you need for your career break is from yourself.

Go ahead, give yourself permission.

Permission to live.

RESOURCES

Accommodation
- AirBnB.com
- BedandBreakfast.com
- CouchSurfing.org
- FlipKey.com
- HomeAway.com
- HouseTrip.com
- HostelBookers.com
- HostelWorld.com
- Hostelling International
- HouseCarers.com
- MindMyHouse.com
- TrustedHousesitters.com

Books in the Traveler's Handbook Series
- *The Food Traveler's Handbook.* Jodi Ettenberg
- *The Luxury Traveler's Handbook.* Sarah and Terry Lee
- *The Solo Traveler's Handbook.* Janice Waugh
- *The Volunteer Traveler's Handbook.* Shannon O'Donnell

Career Break and Related Books
- *Dream. Save. Do. Start Dreaming and Start Living.* Betsy and Warren Talbot
- *Escape 101. The Four Secrets to Taking a Sabbatical or Career Break Without Losing Your Money or Your Mind.* Dan Clements
- *How To Take a Career Break to Travel.* Alexis Grant
- *How to Become a Housesitter and See the World.* Dalene and Pete Heck
- *The Lost Girls: Three Friends. Four Continents. One Unconventional Detour Around the World.* Jennifer Baggett, Holly C. Corbett & Amanda Pressner
- *Negotiating Your Sabbatical. The Ultimate Toolkit for Writing and Presenting a Killer Sabbatical Proposal Your Boss Can't Refuse.* Barbara Pagano, Elizabeth Pagano and Gloria Southerland.
- *Reboot Your Life: Energize Your Career and life by Taking a Break.* Catherine Allen, Nancy Bearg, Rita Foley, Jaye Smith
- *Two Laps Around the World. Tales and Insights from a Life Sabbatical.* Bob Riel
- *Vagabonding: Vagabonding: An Uncommon Guide to the Art of Long-Term World Travel.* Rolf Potts

Career Break TV and Films

- *The Career Break Travel Show* - Global TV show hosted by Jeff Jung, The Career Break Travel Guy. Each episode will take you to a different locale to learn something new, give back through volunteering or take a path less traveled to really experience "the road". You'll see the sites, hear in-depth interviews, and get Jeff's Top Secrets for creating your own adventure and how to make it count.
- *A Map For Saturday.* Earthchild Productions, 2008. Documentary filmed over the course of a year from around the world by Brook Silva-Braga, interviewing people on their career break or gap year.

Other Career Break Resources

- CareerBreakSecrets.com - The independent blog and travel site by author Jeff Jung, The Career Break Travel Guy.
- MeetPlanGo.com - Online prep course, blog and live events in North America to help people prepare for their trip
- YourSabbatical.com - Blog and tools for helping people take their breaks.
- Legalnomads.com (Resources Page)

Budgeting and Money Management

- BudgetYourTrip.com - Has basic cost information and a handy calculator for a variety of destinations.
- RTWexpenses.com
- ThePointsGuy.com - How to get the most out of loyalty programs.
- TravelHacking.org - A service that helps you with travel hacking.
- Xpenser.com - An expense tracker and management tool.

Connecting with Locals and other Travelers

- CouchSurfing.org - Many people use CouchSurfing.org as a means of connecting with locals even if they are not using couchsurfing for accommodation.
- Hermail.net - An international directory of women travelers.
- Meetup.com - Find groups that share your interests (food, politics, wine, knitting, architecture, etc.) and are holding meetings in your destination city.

- Trekkingpartners.com - Find partners to trek and hike all over the world.
- WomenWelcomeWomen.org.uk - 5W is a network of about 2,400 women in over 80 countries ready to help other women with their travels.

Find Great Dining Experiences
- Chowhound.com - A community for foodies with discussions sorted by location. This is a great resource for finding foodies' favorite restaurants in most major cities.
- FoodbyCountry.com - A little bit of history, an overview of food and some recipes.
- GlobalTableAdventure.com - Travel, food, photos and recipes.
- Legalnomads.com - Blog by the author of *The Food Traveler's Handbook*.

Flights
- Airninja.com - Flight search
- Airtreks.com - Multi-stop international itineraries
- Hipmunk.com - Flight search
- For classic round-the-world tickets: OneWorld.com, SkyTeam.com, StarAlliance.com

Health and Health Insurance Resources
- IMG (International Medical Group)
- InsureMytrip.com
- International Red Cross
- International Red Crescent
- Local health insurance broker of choice
- Medex.com
- Squaremouth.com,
- Travel guard
- WorldNomads

Re-entry Resources
- iRelaunch
- LinkedIn
- Local alumni organizations

- Meetup
- Couchsurfing.org
- Local trade association groups
  - Network
  - Alumni associations
  - Meetup
  - Couchsurfing

Registering Your Trip
- Australia: Smartraveller.gov.au/
- Canada: Voyage.gc.ca/
- Ireland: dfa.ie (Under Citizen Services)
- New Zealand: Safetravel.govt.nz/
- United States: State.gov/travel
- United Kingdom: fco.gov.uk (Under Travel & Living Abroad section)

Free Blogging Options
- TravelBlog.org
- TravelPod.com
- GetJealous.com
- Blogger.com
- WordPress.com
- Tumblr.com
- Google Voice
- Skype

Travel Blogs
- CareerBreakSecrets.com
- SoloTravelerBlog.com
- ALittleAdrift.com
- LegalNomads.com
- LiveShareTravel.com

Travel Blog Lists

- ArtofTravelBlogging.com
- BrendansAdventures.com
- Invesp.com/Blog-Rank
- NomadicSamuel.com
- TravMonkey.com

Travel Forums

- AFAR.com - Online community to help get advice from travelers who have been where you're going
- Boards.bootsnall.com - Boots 'n All
- Facebook.com/careerbreaksecrets - Travel community for Career Break Secrets and The Career Break Travel Show
- Fodors.com/community - Fodor's travel forum
- Gogobot.com - Online planning community to help get advice from travelers who have been where you're going
- Lonelyplanet.com/thorntree - Thorntree on Lonely Planet
- MatadorNetwork.com/Community - Matador's community
- Tripadvisor.com - Search the site for Solo Travel Forum for excellent discussions.

Travel Tech Resources

- TooManyAdaptors.com - Travel blog with independent reviews, tips and advice
- *The Ultimate Tech Guide for Travelers* - ebook with tech tips, tricks, and hacks for travelers

Other Useful tools

- AllSubway travel app - Subway maps for cities around the world
- Flashlight app - Turns your smartphone into a flashlight
- Maps.Google.com/streetview - A tool for checking out a neighborhood before you go
- iTunes - There are hundreds of free apps for translation, maps and travel information.

- Oanda.com - Currency conversion tool
- SitorSquat.com - Tells you where the nearest bathrooms are and what they're like.
- TripAdvisor.com - Travelers' reviews of accommodation and more. (To be taken with a grain of salt as reviews can be planted.)
- Tripit - Manages your basic travel information in one place.

Volunteering
- GrassrootsVolunteering.org
- Voluntourism.org
- VolunteerGlobal.com
- WWOOF.org

Endnotes

[1] John Hughes. "Ferris Bueller's Day Off." Paramount Pictures. 1986.

[2] O.B. Davidson, D. Eden, M. Westman, Y. Cohen-Charash, L.B. Hammer, A.N. Kluger, M. Krausz, C. Maslach, M. O'Driscoll, P.L. Perrewé, J.C. Quick, Z. Rosenblatt, P.E. Spector, *"Sabbatical Leave: Who Gains and How Much?"* Journal of Applied Psychology 95, no. 5 (2010)

Jeff Jung

Known as the Career Break Travel Guy, Jeff is host of the new global TV show, *The Career Break Travel Show* and the publisher of *CareerBreakSecrets.com*. He is the leading career break expert in the world and has appeared internationally on TV and radio, in print and online talking about the various issues related to career breaks. An international traveler since his first trip to Australia at the age of sixteen, his career break made him a true citizen of the world. He left a fantastic consulting-turned-corporate marketing career to become fluent in Spanish in South America, see magnificent sunrises in far-flung places like the Galapagos Islands and the Nile River, and learn to ski.

Jeff Jung

Jeff Jung

CPSIA information can be obtained at www.ICGtesting.com
Printed in the USA
BVIW12n1545140917
494789BV00010B/86